How to Read the Bible to Hear God Speak

A study in Numbers 22-24

How to Read the Bible to Hear God Speak

A study in Numbers 22-24

---

a newly expanded edition

Calvin G. Seerveld

Dordt College Press and Toronto Tuppence Press

Printed in the United States of America.

Dordt College Press
498 Fourth Avenue NE
Sioux Center, IA 51250
United States of America
ISBN: 0-932914-50-0
www.dordt.edu/dordt_press

Toronto Tuppence Press
332 Senlac Road
Toronto, Ontario M2R 1R3
Canada
ISBN: 0-919071-08-2
www.seerveld.com/tuppence.html
ttp@icscauada.edu

United States Library of Congress Control Number: 2003109770

National Library of Canada Cataloguing in Publication
Seerveld, Calvin, 1930-
How to read the Bible to hear God speak : a study in Numbers 22-24 / Calvin G. Seerveld. — Newly expanded ed.
Previously published under title: Balaam's apocalyptic prophecies.

1. Balaam, the prophet. 2. Bible. O.T. Numbers XXII-XXIV—Criticism, interpretation, etc. I. Title.

BS580.B3S44 2003 222'.1406
C2003-904363-0

Cover art "Christ among the Children" (1910)
by Emil Nolde, Museum of Modern Art, New York, USA
Cover design by Krista Krygsman
Copy layout by Angela Kevan and Denae Wittmeier

with love

for Anya, Gioia, Luke, Jan and Ian
and for Ben, Mary, and Hannah

to ponder in their heart

Contents

Foreword

The original lectures were titled *Understanding the Scripture: How to read and not to read the Bible* (Toronto: Association for the Advancement of Christian Scholarship, 1968). When they were reprinted, only the title was changed (against my wishes) to *Balaam's Apocalyptic Prophecies: A study in reading Scripture* (Toronto: Wedge Publishing Foundation, 1980). They are here being published unchanged again except for excising any gender references to God. The title now is a good one, closer to the original: *How to Read the Bible to Hear God Speak: A study in Numbers 22-24.* An Afterword with an appendix is newly written.

The ordinary Bible reader in North America probably has no idea that printing and reading a Bible in English was forbidden in England during the reign of Tudor Queen Mary (1553-1558). That is why English Protestants went to Geneva at the time of John Calvin, which led to "The Breeches Bible" translation (1560), the one Shakespeare used during the reign of Queen Elizabeth (1558-1603). For many North American believers today the Bible has become domesticated, like a family pet. The Bible is no longer a wild fire, and it will not cost you your life if you are caught reading it in Michigan, California, New Jersey, Texas, or Canada.

But do we know how to read the Bible as it is written rather than make it say what lets us feel comfortable?

It is so that a person may hear different accents of the Bible depending upon whether you are the mechanic under the car fixing it or the fellow who owns the Mercedes. It is also true that Bible reading has often been misused to justify power trips: ancient Israel used its special access to the Word of God spoken to Abraham (Genesis 12:1-3) to presume its election with God was irrevocable (Matthew 3:7-10). The Church under Pope Urban II (1088-98) and Innocent III (1198-1216) championed crusades—"It is God's will!"—to wage war as knights of the cross to police pilgrims' safety to visit and control "the holy land," with disastrous results. Europeans liberated from persecution by coming to the "promised land" of North America were tempted to think of themselves as God's chosen people and authorized to treat indigenous native Americans as if they were the Canaanites to be conquered or gotten rid of. And is it not a shame upon the one body of Christ that an African nation today may sport 50 splintered denominations of churches because Christians read the Bible in divergent ways?

But we still need to read the Bible, together.

This booklet wants to pull anybody who picks it up back to the source of communal renewal: God's living Word. The flourishing existence of Islam around the world today may be a judgment of God on the state of christianity. We Christians have too frequently done what seems right in our own groupie eyes (Judges 17:6), we go with the flow of whatever fashionable cultural currents are in force. The Bible, however, has an everlasting unchangeableness about it, provides us a centering orientation, points to a sure place to stand—Jesus Christ's compassionate Rule—and promises to bring faithful Bible readers to a healing maturity and ministry in the power of the Holy Spirit, despite persecution (Hebrews 5:11-6:8, Matthew 5:48, 6:25-33, Mark 10:23-31). The Holy Scriptures are the place where God speaks: we are called to do the hearing.

I am grateful for the opportunity to send this little loaf of bread out once more upon the waters (Ecclesiastes 11:1-6).

Toronto
Pentecost 2003 A.D.

Preface

More than ten years ago certain believing students and teachers, workers and housewives asked the Association for the Advancement of Christian Scholarship to have someone speak to them about how to read the Bible. Bible reading is not so easy when you are accustomed to snippets of newscasts and short digested articles in weekly news magazines. The Bible is a longer book, and holds together. The hurried pace of North American life and the brief exposure to a few verses in a sermon once a week do not help so much either. Bible reading takes time and knowing how, if you want to do it right. And that is what certain people of God in Canada were interested in.

The following pages of print record lectures that tried to respond to that concern. The lectures were carefully researched and prayed through, because reading the Bible is a gut issue. I am convinced that many a Christian goes to the Bible with good intentions, and still comes away with a mangled Word of God, missing the riches of its proclamation. How can a man or a woman, educated or not, go to the Scriptures with an imaginative, childlike trust, hear its storied Truth freshly so that it re-form his or her whole lifetime of activity and bear fruit worthy of our LORD rather than inhibit our creatureliness? I have tried to show a way to go that works out of a vital tradition that took shape in the sixteenth-century Reformation of the church and societal life.

In my own communion, the Christian Reformed Church of North America, we "believe without any doubt all things contained in the holy Scriptures . . . especially because the Holy Spirit witnesses in our hearts that they are from God" (*Belgic Confession of Faith*, article 5, formulated in 1561 by Guido de Brès, adopted by the Synod of Dordt as a doctrinal standard, 1618-19). This is my committed starting point.

During several long, friendly talks with certain Baptist pastors in the Chicago area of the United States during the 1960s it became clear to me that believing the Bible is the infallible Word of God is not enough for understanding the Scriptures aright. You can totally trust the stoplight's green, yellow, and red to tell you what to do, but you still might be colour-blind and miss the signals. I also began to sense how crucial it is to have "the whole counsel of God" and the whole history narrated from Genesis to Revelation ever percolating in your consciousness as you read a smaller portion of Scripture. Reading and interpreting the Bible piecemeal does violence to its integrity as a single, unified text. Treating the Bible, wittingly or not, as a patchwork quilt of oracles or fragments or homilies encourages everyone to indulge his or her whims.

If I were to state simply what I believe is the key to understanding the Bible, so I could avoid scrutinizing it like a Pharisee or Sadducee scribe (cf. Luke 11:52, John 5:36-40), I would say something like this: one needs to realize that the holy Scriptures are God-speaking literature given to us historically for our learning by faith the one true story of the LORD's Rule acoming and the contours of our obedient response. I believe the holy Scriptures come at us as the compelling Word of the LORD and that it faces us whole, bodily men and women in our concrete life activity today with the overall directive to praise the LORD!, repent and get adopted!, love your neighbour as yourself, and reconcile all creation back to God in Jesus Christ! It is to this ministry of thankfulness for what God has done for fallen creation in Jesus Christ that the LORD calls us through the Scriptures (cf. II Corinthians 5:17-21). Every reader and hearer either heartfully accepts and concretely obeys this pregnant directive, in the guiding strength of the Holy Spirit, or lets it pass by, as a fool.

So there are four elements fused in my biblical hermeneutical method, you might say: (1) find the passage's thread in the whole true story narrative of history as God reveals it; (2) discern the literary configuration of the passage you are reading; (3) win a sense of the historical matrix in which the section was booked; (4) listen intently, on your knees as it were, to the convicting enlightening direction-message.

People have different Bibles depending upon what they assume (1) to be—what is the main, true story of the Bible. (I go to Acts 1:3 for my lead.) One must always remember that no correct formula and not even the right perspective for Bible reading guarantees you sound exegesis every time. We believing men and women readers are fallible. The Bible's kerygmatic nature (4) defies a paint-by-number kind of exposition. Each portion of Scripture has to be prayerfully wrestled with in the communion of the saints under the leading of the Holy Spirit as to its historical matrix (3) and its literary contours (2) within the defining limits of (1) and (4). (I begin with Luke 24:44 and Hebrews 1:1 for orientation on the kind of narrative and the reality of historical date to the biblical text.) The final understanding of a passage—detecting the point of the piece, in the context of the whole Bible, for our lives now—is always an understanding of Scripture that is an accountable, existential understanding that shall bear good fruit in season or hurt people with its misleading lie. (I struggle to be responsible for the blessing promised in Proverbs 1:2-6 and II Timothy 3:16-17.)

What follows is a case study of reading Numbers 22-24. I try to show how different stances assumed on the critical hermeneutical issues affect the understanding of this Bible passage. I try to do it popularly but with professional care. Except for a few typographical corrections, the lectures reprinted here are exactly as they appeared in 1968. They are presented again in the spirit of diaconal service.

> *"Do you also understand what you are reading?" asked Philip.*
>
> *"How could I," answered the Ethiopian eunuch, "unless somebody takes the trouble to lead me into it." (Acts 8:30-31)*

I have tried to take the trouble to lead fellow believers and any curious disbelievers into understanding the Scriptures they read in Numbers 22-24, and I pray that God will bless what has been done right, because only in God's written Word can one find the direction for life.

Toronto, June 1979

Palestine

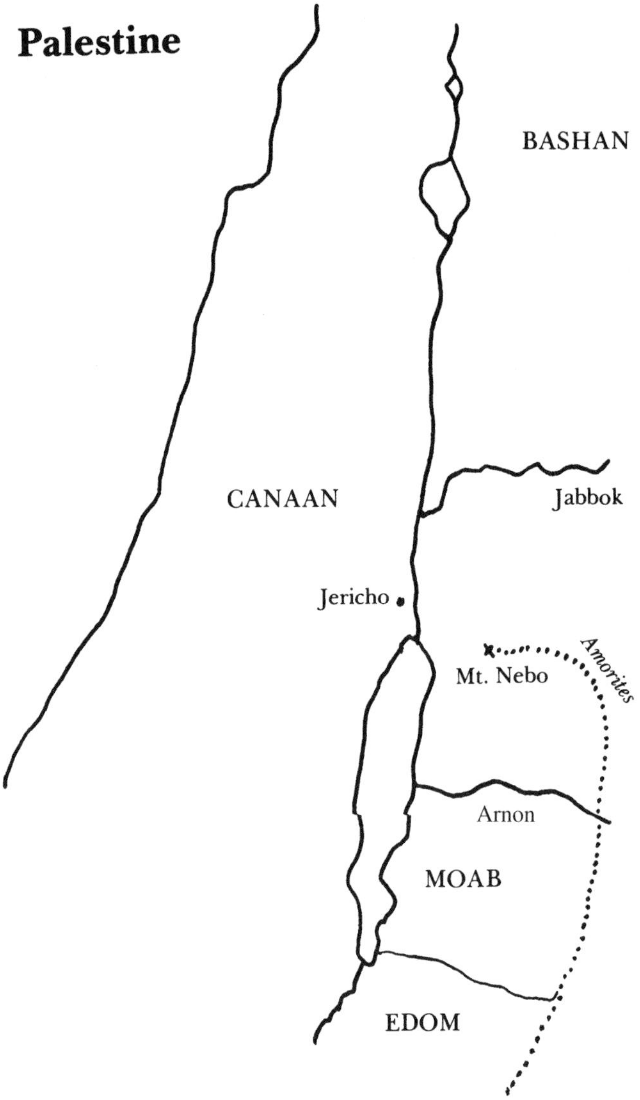
BASHAN
CANAAN
Jabbok
Jericho
Amorites
Mt. Nebo
Arnon
MOAB
EDOM

Reading Numbers 22-24

Rather than talk about how to read and not to read the Bible, I think we should begin by doing it together, and then reflect on the ways it can be done compared to what we are doing.

We shall read Numbers 22-24.

The Israelites are still being brought up out of Egypt-land by the LORD God Yahweh. They are circling in on Canaan now after almost forty years of wandering in the wilderness (cf. Numbers 14), around the Sinai peninsula. They have just tiptoed around Edom (descendants of Esau), skirted the eastern border of Moab (descendants of Lot), without touching a single vineyard or field of grain.

Amorites had captured part of what used to be northern Moab. May we pass peacefully through your territory, on the main caravan highway, to Canaan?, asked the people under Moses. The Amorite chieftain Sihon said No, and he came out into the wilderness to attack (Numbers 21:23). God gave God's own people a total victory, so that they conquered the city of Heshbon, near Mount Nebo, and took possession of the land from the Arnon river to the Jabbok.

Then, as the Israelites wandered North into the rich herding land of Bashan, king Og engaged them in battle. But the LORD gave God's people a total victory again, and they took possession of the land of Og (Numbers 21:35).

"Later," says the Word of God (Numbers 22:1), "the children of Israel pulled up stakes, went and settled themselves (southward) in the plains of Moab, on the other (East) side of the Jordan, opposite Jericho."

22 2 When Balak, son of Zippor, got to know everything the
3 Israelites had done to the Amorites, a sickening fear of
(God's) people got hold of Moab—there were so many,
many of them; Moab dreaded the felt presence of the
children of Israel.

22 **Moab** (to the grey-haired elders of Midian):
4 *This horde is set to devour everything around us like the ox crushes to pulp fresh green plants of the field.*

5 So Balak, son of Zippor, who was king of Moab at that time, sent messengers to Balaam, son of Beor, at Pethor, which is on the (Euphrates) river, to call him up out of the land of his countrymen.

King Balak (instructing messengers):
Say—
Look here, a folk come up out of Egyptland!
Look here!, it blankets the earth so far as an eye can see;
it has settled itself down directly opposite me!
6 *Come now, please, and*
weave an evil spell for me upon this folk
for it is overwhelming me—
Perhaps then I might strike it a blow
and drive it out of the land,
for I know that
Whoever you bless is gifted with choice powers
but whoever you place a spell upon is cursed. . . .

7 Then the grey-haired elders of Moab and the grey-haired elders of Midian made the trip, the customary fee for soothsaying in their hand. When they reached Balaam, they spoke the words of Balak to him.

Balaam (to the distinguished envoys):
8 *Spend the night here.*
I shall bring you word tomorrow
whatever Word Yahweh speaks to me.

So the official ambassadors of Moab stayed with Balaam. (That night) God came to Balaam.

22 **God:**
9 *Who are these men with you?*

Balaam:

10 *Balak, son of Zippor, king of Moab, has approached me—*
11 *"Look here!, the folk that is coming up out of Egyptland!,*
they blanket the earth as far as an eye can see!
Come now, denounce it for me—
perhaps then I can box it in and get rid of it."

God:

12 *Do not go along with them (Balaam).*
Never curse that folk!
for it is a specially blessed people.

13 Balaam got up the next morning and spoke with the envoys of Balak.

Balaam:

Journey back to your land because Yahweh has refused to let me go along with you.

14 So the official ambassadors of Moab set out (for home) and came to Balak.

Envoys (to Balak):

Balaam refused to travel with us.

15 But Balak still went ahead, dispatched official messengers, many more and more distinguished than the first ones. They arrived where Balaam was.

Ambassadors (to Balaam):

16 *Balak, son of Zippor, wishes said to you,*
"Please do not let yourself be hindered from traveling my way.
17 *I can honour, reward, distinguish you extraordinarily!*
22 *Anything you say to me I will do.*
So come now, please, and speak evil over this folk for me."

Balaam (responding to those who served Balak):

18 *If Balak were to give me his house full of silver and gold, I still could not violate what the mouth of my God Yahweh speaks, whether the deed were to be a trifle or something significant.*

19 *However, since you are here now too, settle down, won't you, for tonight so that I may find out what else Yahweh means to say to me.*

20 God came to Balaam in the night.

God:

Since the men have come to call you away, get up.
Go ahead with them.
But make certain (Balaam) you enact only the Word that I speak to you.

21 After Balaam got up the next morning he saddled his she-ass and went along with the official ambassadors of Moab.

22 God's face began to get red with indignation, because
going on the journey Balaam certainly was! So the Angel
of Yahweh set himself square in the way to be Balaam's
adversary while he was happily riding along on his she-
23 ass, two helpers with him. When the ass saw the Angel of
Yahweh standing square in the way, his sword drawn out
ready in his hand, the ass slanted off the road and started
walking through the cultivated field, so that Balaam struck
24 the ass a blow to get it back on the track. Then the Angel
of Yahweh went to where the way was a narrow corridor
between two vineyards, wall on one side and wall on the
other side, and set himself up there square in the middle.
22 25 When the ass saw the Angel of Yahweh (there) she tried
to squeeze past close to the hard stone barrier, but she
squashed Balaam's foot against the stone. So Balaam
26 took up hitting and striking the she-ass more blows!
Yahweh's Angel kept it up, going on ahead a ways, and
took a stand in such a narrow spot you could not veer a
27 bit to left or right. When the she-ass saw the Angel of
Yahweh again, she collapsed flat on the ground under
Balaam. Balaam's face got red with indignation; he beat
28 and beat the ass with the hard walking stick. Then Yahweh
opened the mouth of the ass so that she could speak to

Balaam.

Ass:

What have I done to you to make you club me now three times?

Balaam (to the ass):

29 *It is because you have played me for a fool!*
If a sword were in my hand, you would already be a dead beast!

Ass:

30 *Am I not your she-ass that you have ridden upon since you were practically born to this very day?*
Have I been accustomed ever to do to you what I have just been doing?

Balaam:

31 *No, (it is true.)*

With that, Yahweh unveiled Balaam's eyes so that he saw the Angel of Yahweh standing still in the way, his sword drawn out ready in his hand. And Balaam fell to his knees and threw himself flat on his face.

22 **Angel of Yahweh** (to Balaam):

32 *Why did you club your ass now three times?*
Look here, it is I who did the work of hindering antagonist, because the trip has been making my stomach turn!
33 *The ass saw me and veered away from me these three times.*
If she had not turned aside, why you, yes, you! would already be a dead man, and I would have let the beast alive.

Balaam (to the Angel of Yahweh):

34 *I have done wrong.*
I did not know that You had taken a stand to thwart my passage.

But if it strikes you now as objectionable, I shall betake myself home.

Angel of Yahweh (to Balaam):

35 *Go ahead with the men.*
However, nothing but the Word that I speak to you—
only that Word may you speak.

So there went Balaam, jogging along with the official ambassadors of Balak.

36 When Balak heard that Balaam was acoming, he set out to meet him at the border city of Moab called Arnon, on the extreme edge of Moabite territory.

King Balak (upon meeting Balaam):

37 *Did I not go all out with my invitation to get you here?*
Why have you not come to me (earlier)?
Really! Am I not able to make you an honoured man?!

Balaam (to Balak):

38 *Well, here I am now, come to you.*
But do I have any power at all to say even anything?
The Word that God puts in my mouth:
only that Word may I speak.

22 39 Then Balaam went along with Balak till they came to a
40 (decent) town with streets. There Balak slaughtered cattle,
sheep and goats for a sacrifice of fellowship; he presented (portions of the meat) to Balaam and the noble envoys who had accompanied him.

41 Right the next morning it was that Balak had Balaam fetched and led him away up to some holy hill places of Baal, from where he could spy an outskirt of "that folk."

23 **Balaam** (to Balak after viewing the scene and location):

1 *Build me seven altars here; and fix me up, right here, seven young bulls and seven strong rams.*

2 Balak did just as Balaam said. So there you had it: Balak and Balaam too! offering a bull and a ram on each altar.

Balaam (to Balak):

3 *You stay here tending your sacrifice till it is burned completely to ashes,*
while I take a little walk.
Perhaps Yahweh will cross my path.
No matter what omen he lets me experience I shall make it known to you.

So Balaam took a walk to a spot on the hill that was bare
4 of trees. And God crossed his path there.

Balaam (to God):
The seven altars I got all set up in order!
And I sacrificed a bull and a ram on each one!

5 But Yahweh put a saying in Balaam's mouth.

Yahweh:
You go back to Balak, and you speak what has been told you.

6 So Balaam went back to Balak and look here!, there he
23 7 was, standing over his burning sacrifice, King Balak!,
and all the princely officials of Moab. As he approached,
Balaam raised his voice and spoke the saying formulated
for him.

Balaam (to the assemblage):
Out of Mesopotamia Balak led me on.
King of Moab guided me out of mountains in the Orient.
"Come, cast a spell for me upon Jacob!
Come, invoke destruction—maledict (this) Israel!"

8 *How shall I speak evil of one whom God has not denounced?*
How could I menace with threats one whom Yahweh has not cursed!

9 *Yes, I am seeing it from the top of rocky cliffs!*
I behold it, indeed!, from these very hills. . . .
Look!, a folk that settles itself securely off to the side,
and does not reckon itself as just one of the peoples of the world.

10 *Who can count up the sand grains of Jacob?*
Who could count out even a quarter of Israel's number?
May I die the death of such right living ones.
May what finally happens to me be like the final
(glorious) days of that folk!—

Balak (to Balaam):

11 *What have you done to me!?*
I had you brought here to damn my enemies with curses!
And look now what you have done!
You blessed (them), blessed (them)!!

Balaam (answering Balak):

12 *Do I not have to take extreme care to speak only the*
Word that Yahweh puts in my mouth?

Balak (to Balaam):

13 *Come now, please, with me to a different place;*
23 *there you can see it too—*
only its fringe will you see, you shall not see all of it—
14 *but denounce it for me from there.*

Then Balak took Balaam along with him up to a field full of watchtowers at the top of the Pisgah mountain range. There too he built seven altars and again began offering a bull and offering a ram on each altar.

Balaam (to Balak):

15 *You stand here and take care of matters connected with*
your burning sacrifice,
but I—let me try to come across something like before. . . .

16 And Yahweh did cross Balaam's path, and God put a saying in Balaam's mouth.

Yahweh:

You go back to Balak, and you speak what has been told you.

17 When Balaam arrived where Balak was, look at that!, there he was, bending over his smoking sacrifice, surrounded by princely officials of Moab.

Balak (catching sight of Balaam):
18 *What did Yahweh speak?*

In answer, Balaam raised his voice and spoke the saying formulated for him.

Balaam (to the assemblage):
Stand up, Balak, and listen, listen!
Prick up your ears for me, you son of Zippor!
19 *God is not a man that God would go back on God's word!*
God is no son of a man that lets himself be cajoled!
23 *Has God ever said something God did not bring about?*
Has God ever spoken a Word that God did not complete?
20 *Do you understand? For blessing I was engaged:*
God has declared a blessing! and I cannot undo it.
21 *God has not stared at Jacob's deceit.*
God has not looked at Israel's troublesomeness.
Yahweh, their God, is right in with them!
Victory shouting celebrating a king is part of their life!
22 *God who is bringing them up out of Egyptland*
protects them like the strong horns of a wild ox.
23 *Indeed, there is no black magic in Jacob;*
There is no sorcery in Israel at all.
At the right time Jacob is spoken to,
Israel is told what God has been doing!
24 *What a folk! It rears up like a lioness!*
It springs high in the air like a male lion!
It does not lie down to sleep till it has eaten prey,
till it has drunk blood of those it has killed.

Balak (cutting off Balaam):
25 *Cursing, you do not denounce it!*
Then also blessing, you may not gift it with powers!

Balaam (answering Balak directly):
26 *Have I not told you,*
"Everything that Yahweh speaks,
that is what I perform."

Balak (persisting, tiring):
27 *Come along now, please,*
I shall conduct you to one other place.
Perhaps it will suit God that you perform an
incantation for me over it from there.

28 So Balak led Balaam away, way out and up to the moun-
tainous Peor's summit, panoramically overlooking the
23 whole stretch of forsaken wilderness below.

Balaam (to Balak):
29 *Build me seven altars here; and*
fix me up, right here, seven young bulls and seven
strong rams.

30 Balak did again just as Balaam said to do. And he went
about sacrificing a bull and a ram on each altar.
24 1 Since Balaam now finally sensed that it pleased
Yahweh to have Israel blessed, he did not go for a walk
like other times, in the chance of coming across omens,
2 but turned his face toward the bleak desert. When he
raised his eyes, Balaam saw Israel; he saw Israel settled
3 clearly according to tribal divisions. Then it happened:
God's Spirit came upon him, and Balaam raised his voice
and spoke the saying formulated for him.

Balaam (to the assemblage, while envisioning the Israelites stretched out on the plain):
So speaks Balaam, the son of Beor!
So speaks the big man whose eye was shut!
4 *So speaks one who is listening to the speaking of God!*
Who is seeing a vision of the Almighty One!
—crestfallen, but eyes unveiled . . .
5 *How beautiful are your tents, 0 Jacob!*
How lovely your flimsy homes, 0 Israel!
6 *like undulating valley river beds they roll into the distance,*
like gardens (lush) by riverside,
like thick, rich tufted herbs Yahweh has planted,
like cedar-smelling woods near brooks. . . .

7 *(I see) him spilling water overflowing from his drawn leathern bucket:*
Jacob's seed shall always be moist with more than enough water.
(I see) a king in Israel!, looming large above Agag—
24 *The majestic rule of Israel shall (continually) expand, be exalted!*
8 *God who is bringing Jacob up out of Egyptland*
protects them like the strong horns of a wild ox:
God eats up peoples who threaten it!
God tramples their bones to bits!
God destroys whoever plagues it!
9 *Israel rests like a lion in his lair, lain down for sleep,*
like a lioness! Who dare disturb it?
Whoever invokes blessings upon you shall be blessed;
Whoever invokes evil upon you shall be cursed!

10 Then Balak's face got red with indignation at Balaam, and he hit his hands together—

Balak (to Balaam):
I called you out here to damn my enemies with curses!
And what has happened?
You have blessed!, given a blessing three times!
11 *Get you to your own place quick!*
I planned to distinguish you with extraordinary honour,
but—there it is!—(your) Yahweh has kept you from such glory.

Balaam (answering Balak):
12 *Yet, did I not?, remember, talk with your messengers,*
the ones you dispatched to where I was, and say,
"If Balak were to give me his house full of silver and gold,
13 *I still could not violate what the mouth of Yahweh speaks,*
even if I wanted to pronounce something good or something bad—
nothing but the Word that Yahweh speaks,
only that Word may I speak!"?

[14] *So I am already journeying back to my people,*
do you see?
But you "come now," (and) I will tell you something!,
teach you what this folk shall finally do to your folk in the last days!

24 [15] Once more Balaam raised his voice and spoke the saying formulated for him.

Balaam (entranced by the future):
[16] *So speaks Balaam, the son of Beor!*
So speaks the big man whose eye was shut!
So speaks one who is listening to the speaking of God!
Who is discovering what the Most High One knows!
Who is seeing a vision of the Almighty One!
—crestfallen, but eyes unveiled . . .
[17] *I see him!, but he is not yet there.*
I am really seeing him!!, but he is not close enough—
A shooting star come from Jacob!
A majestic meteor from Israel is poised aloft:
it has demolished both flanks of Moab!
it has shattered and ruined all, yes, all the sons of Seth!
[18] *Jacob's enemies—*
Edom has become a piece of property;
Seir too has become possessed land:
It is Israel that is gaining productive power!
[19] *(The one I see) shall take command from out of Jacob*
and shall devastate anyone who deserts the city . . . .

[20] Then Balaam saw Amalek (in a vision), raised his voice and spoke the saying formulated for him:

Balaam:
Amalek—first of the peoples (attacking Jacob)?
Very well: utter destruction shall meet it at last.

[21] Then Balaam saw the Kenites (living with Israel), raised his voice and spoke the saying formulated for him:

Balaam:

So secure is the place you dwell in;
Your nest is nestled in a rocky crag.
22 *But if the Kenite had removal in store,*
How long would it be (before) Assyria took you captive?

24 23 For the last time Balaam raised his voice and spoke a saying formulated for him:

Balaam:

Woe to you who are still alive when God executes all this!
24 *Ships from the Cyprian coast shall humiliate Assyria*
and their far-flung descendants;
But also (that tormenting people) shall sink into
nothing. . . .

25 With that, Balaam stood up and began his journey to go back to the place where he came from. Balak too went his way.

Standard Ways of Reading Scripture

This literal translation—check it with your King James or Revised Standard Version—has been carefully prepared to teach those who can hear something important about reading the Bible. Before I explain and develop what is behind this kind of proposal for reform in reading the Scriptures, we should get clear what other, standard ways there are of reading the Bible. When people in our western civilization have opened this book to Numbers 22, if they seriously took the section through to the end of chapter 24, how would they read or have they read it?

A fundamentalistic reading

One straightforward, simple way often taken in Bible reading wants to know what lessons we can learn from this unusual story of Balaam, Balak, ass, angel and all. What is God telling you and me through this infallible and inspired revelation that can point us to heaven and keep us from the Evil One?

This way of reading would go something like this:

The double-dealing character of Balaam is very revealing. He knows the LORD, even by several names—God, Yahweh, Almighty One (24:4)—and he does not respond to the Moabite delegation before he first seeks the will of the LORD; but deep down he is driven throughout by a strong passion for the earthly honour Balak has promised. Once confronted by the tents of Jacob, he says almost spontaneously, "Let me die the death of the righteous, and let my last end be like his!" (23:10); yet he keeps on seeking permission to curse Israel.

He wants the best of two worlds that are incompatible. He is willing to die righteous, but not to live righteously. And that is something God will not allow. If you have the gift of prophecy, understand mysteries, and have all kinds of knowledge (I Corinthians 13:2), but do not obey God and love God's people, what does it profit you? You must be doers of God's Will; not knowers and wishers and hearers only (James 1:22).

Balaam always halted between two opinions, and he who hesitates is lost. When the second, more illustrious delegation came, probably with many more gifts, Balaam said, "No, if Balak gave me his house full of gold, I could not go against the Word of Yahweh; nevertheless, stay overnight, and I'll see what I can do." That is exactly how Satan tempts us! He gets us to play with fire, look for a loophole in what we know to be right, doublecross our conscience.

Balaam should have answered what Abraham resolutely told the king of Sodom, "I have sworn to God to take none of your goods so that no one may say you instead of the LORD made Abraham rich" (Genesis 14:22-23). But the lure of prosperity and earthly glory was too great for the soothsayer Balaam. II Peter says (2:15) "he loved the wages of unrighteousness." He wanted to have his piety and eat it too, in luxury; but because the love of money is the root of all evil (I Timothy 6:10), and Balaam succumbed to that love, his end was evil, impious harm to God's people (cf. Numbers 25; 31:16), and sorrow for himself. Compromise, in the christian experience, always leads to sin and misery.

This Scripture is profitable, of course, for instructing us in all manner of righteousness. The fact that Balaam scrupulously offered sacrifices of seven bulls and seven rams, meticulously, and had his prophecies phrased poetically, with impressive oracular form (24:3-4, 15-16), only goes to prove how easy it is to have the form of godliness but to deny the power thereof (II Timothy 3:5). The direct message JESUS SAVES does not need ritual or flowery language to be effective. Genuine worship of God will shun everything showy as if it be the devil. Believers must not seem, but be.

The fact that Balaam's ass reproved him for the beatings teaches us that God wants nothing of his creation abused. If asses, ravens, and whales could talk today, how might not the ears of us ring! As Paul says in Romans 8 (verses 19-23): All creation, the whole plant and animal kingdom, groan!, burdened by the abusive sin of us men, waiting for the second coming of Christ. Next time you are troubled by polluted air, ravaged forests, diseased meat, do not curse the elements and creatures, but look to yourself, slow to anger (James 1:19), humbled by your human misuse of God's world.

Above all, though, what this portion of God's Word holds out to us who read it is the solemn lesson of Balaam's double-dealing life and bitter death, justly executed by Moses with the captured kings of Midian (Numbers 31:8). Balaam reached for two worlds, the earthly and the heavenly, and lost both: you cannot serve God and Mammon. So if you are caught in the dilemma of Romans 7, doing what you would not and not doing what you would, believe on the LORD Jesus Christ and be saved from your indecision and sins; "resist the devil, and he will flee from you" (James 4:7). And if you are a believer who thinks he or she stands, take heed, remember Balaam, lest you fall: the wages of sin is death (Romans 6:23).

These remarks illustrate, in brief,[1] a way of reading Numbers 22-24 that, to give it a name, I would typify as a fundamentalistic evangelical reading.

A higher-critical reading

A quite different method takes Numbers 22-24 in hand and wants to figure out how this section of text is put together. When could it have been written down, and why? What historical setting does the passage betray? Does it tell us anything significant about Israel's relation to its ethnic contemporaries? Is the text before us reliable? Are there any discrepancies?

With such an intent, critical outlook, the reading would begin something like this:

In 22:12 God says emphatically: Do not go with those men!; but in 22:22 God says: You may go! Did God change God's mind? And then, once Balaam starts going, God gets angry. The whole episode of talking ass and obstructing angel (22:22-34) does not fit the context of the story if God was permitting him to go. Balaam says (22:34): Should I go home then? According to 22:35 the answer is: Keep going to Balak! Thus we are back exactly where we started in 22:20.

There are other odd things too. If Balaam came from Pethor on the Euphrates river in Mesopotamia (that is Aramland; 22:5 and 23:7; cf. Deuteronomy 23:5), he did not travel by ass. That distance from Moab is about a twenty-day camel trip (cf. Genesis 24:10). Why are the elders of Midian mentioned by name (in 22:4,7), then dropped from the story and never heard about again? There are frequently unnecessary, repetitious statements: 22:3b simply repeats 22:3a; Balak gets introduced as the son of Zippor in 22:2, and after a lapse of two verses describing the whole situation, as if we never heard of him before, the end of 22:4 introduces him again as Balak, the son of Zippor, somewhat belatedly, king of Moab.

Such stylistic flaws, minor inconsistencies, and difficulties like "to go or not to go" all point to the fact that various accounts of a Balaam figure and his relation to Moab and Midian and Israel and what happened when Yahweh had the Israelites enter Canaan—various divergent accounts of this famous, foreign, soothsaying prophet circulated for years and years orally before they were put in writing, at different times, until finally someone collected and edited together all the different, extant documents into one finished piece, which is the foundation of our present manuscripts. That is, the so-called contradictions, variants and difficulties for interpretation are not to be explained in terms of biographical flaws in Balaam, for example, but simply as the natural result of editing diverse traditions, editing, let us say, two basic treatments of those fantastic happenings back in the age when God brought Jacob up out of Egyptland, editing distinct strands into one rope. It is a little as if the gospel according to Mark and according to John had been fused by an editor into one book. There would be some overlapping, different emphases, odd fragments, incongruous details, but a single narrative—much like Numbers 22-24.

Proof for the fact that this text originated from quite distinct sources can be shown by careful scrutiny of the four "prophetic sayings" in Balaam's mouth.

Each of the last two (see 24:3-9 and 24:15-19, plus fragments in 24:20-24) begins with this elevating, chanted formula:

Thus speaks Balaam, the son of Beor!
Thus speaks the big man whose eye was shut!
Thus speaks one who is listening to the speaking of God!
Who is seeing a vision of the Almighty One!

after which blessings are spoken:

How lovely are your tents . . .
water overflowing . . .
majestic rule of Israel expanding . . .
like a lion in his lair . . .
I see a shooting star come from Jacob . . .
demolishing all his enemies . . . .

Both these oracles, uttered ecstatically under the indwelling presence of God's Spirit (24:2), have the form of stately benediction, a form that recurs through the Older Testament almost as a genre. When hoary-headed Jacob was practically on his deathbed in Egypt, he called in his sons (Genesis 49:2):

Gather round and listen closely, sons of Jacob!
Listen, listen! to your father Israel—

and then follows a chapter of blessings for Reuben, Simeon and Levi, Judah, Zebulun, Issachar, Dan, Gad, Asher, Naphtali, Joseph, and Benjamin. Deuteronomy 33 reports a similar visionary benediction Moses spoke over the heads of the tribes of Israel just before he expired. When words are spoken as if they have empowering force, grace-giving, official character, then they take on such highly stylized, oracular benedictional form.

These two oracles of Balaam assume in their content no knowledge at all of a Balaam-Balak affair. These last "sayings" do, however, witness to other events: "a king in Israel higher than Agag" (24:7) recalls immediately the business of I Samuel 15 (cf. I Samuel 10:23); and "a shooting star from Jacob . . . demolishing Moab, Edom, Seir" (24:17-18) is a standard way of praising with encomium the Lion of Judah who slew his ten thousands. There is no Messianic prophecy here; you have to read it into the verse to get it there. Jesus Christ of Nazareth never "demolished both flanks of Moab" (24:17), but meteoric king David certainly did (II Samuel 8:2, 14). The whole fighting, celebrating temper of these last sayings fits the time when Agag, Saul, and David maybe were in the news, when Israel was becoming proudly conscious of herself as a mighty nation, with a king, subduing foes in the strength of her God Yahweh.

By contrast, the first two sayings (see 23:1-10 and 23:18-24) both assume an immediate connection with the Balaam-Balak, Moab-Israel confrontation; but they are much more confessionally tuned than politically oriented. Now

Israel does not reckon herself among the (warring)
nations of the world . . .
she dwells securely alone . . .

There is developed theological reflection:

God is not a man who would lie . . .
God is no man that he should repent . . .
God himself is King in the midst of his people . . .

and imagery of battles won in bygone days has the gentle bombast of reminiscing stereotype:

A folk that rears up like a lioness!
It does not sleep till it has eaten prey . . .
till it has drunk blood of those it has killed.

That is not benedictional language or about current events; it has a hymned, retrospective, somewhat resigned cast to the sentiments, a spirit quite close to that of Judah after her brothers, the ten tribes of Israel, had been carried away into Assyrian captivity and Judah herself was no longer a powerhouse.

Careful reading, analysis, makes clear that this passage in Numbers discloses a pattern followed elsewhere in Older Testament biblical writings. The third and fourth oracles were probably composed first, before the kingdom of Solomon divided (early tenth century BC). The vignette of ass and angel of Yahweh that got associated with these oracles drew on an oral tradition about a non-Hebraic, professional soothsayer inspired by divine power, who was also a servant of Yahweh. A different oral tradition concerning Balaam went into the Balaam-Balak account, where a pious man of God, who met God privately at night, in dreams, and after sacrificing, to ask his direction, was enticed by Balak to go against the God he feared. Oracles one and two were composed with this struggle in mind (probably late seventh century BC, just before the fall of Jerusalem). A later editor pulled these pieces of rope together and placed the whole section before chapter 25.[2]

Given this originating formation, it becomes obvious that Numbers 22-24 is not a historical account of exactly what took place once upon a time. Benediction, hymn, combined with the fable of a talking ass—fascinating!, but incredible on any grounds other than folklore. [Notice how the writer of Numbers rationalized beyond the talking snake of Genesis 3, adding "*Yahweh* opened the ass's mouth" (22:28).] Benedictions, hymns, and fable are not the ingredients of precise historiography. The narrative cannot mean to be taken as a historical account: traipsing up and down three different mountain ranges with extensive animal slaughter could hardly have happened in continuous succession as the story portrays it.

More fundamental evidence still of what we are dealing with here shows up in the fact that this whole section assumes a uniform exodus and entry into the Promised Land by a homogeneous band of people. That is saga as far as what we know happened—which Judges 1 reports much more accurately—waves of marauding, Semitic tribes attacking and winning footholds here and there in ancient Canaan. Numbers 22-24 has saga character. That does not mean it is unhistorical; it means it is simply not factual history. It is like the saga of the American Revolution which middle class, white teachers tell their grade school charges—Boston Tea Party . . . the ride of Paul Revere . . . crossing the Potomac river on Christmas Eve—to instill in them patriotic ideals. Saga always has historical connections but is like a colour-tinted, touched-up photograph, a little brighter and more epic than what baldly probably took place. But saga is not worthless fiction.

Important about these chapters before us is that they construct a kind of religiously sensitive, heightened dramatization of the peril Israel was in again at the climax of its journey. Will the forty-year-old fiasco of Kadesh-Barnea somehow be repeated, or will the new generation make it this time? Enemy Moab goes to Israel's jugular vein: they are a blessed people? OK, get them cursed! So they hire the highest-paid Simon Magus of the Orient to do the job. Balaam and Balak as personages are not important; it is the battle between Israel and Moab this whole saga highlights, and that Israel's God Yahweh had the power to defend his people, turning the will to curse into an act of blessing.[3]

One more thing needs to be noticed: Numbers 22-24 does not fault Balaam for inordinate greed (cf. 22:18; 24:12-13). It was the most ordinary thing in the world to receive payment for soothsaying services (Saul and his servant needed money to pay the "seer" Samuel for telling them where to find the lost asses of his father; I Samuel 9:5-10). The significance of Balaam—besides the fact that the account incidentally reveals what the Hebrew writer understood a true prophet of Yahweh to be: one who, even against his will, faithfully brings the words that the LORD says he should speak—the relevance of Balaam is that here you have an outright heathen used by God to make God's will known. That is, Scripture is approving the idea that unbelievers can be vehicles of the truth, that magi from the East, outside the pale of God's people, can bear a *testimonium animae naturaliter Christianae*, that Sartre's *No Exit* and *The Graduate* film can possibly witness more to God's Law than a phony Sunday school sermonette, and that it will be a vicious church that thinks it has a monopoly on God's prophetic wisdom and does not recognize revelation wherever it can be found.

This kind of exacting, thorough, spirited inquiry into Numbers 22-24 constitutes what I should call a scholarly humanistic reading.

A dogmatic reading

One other standard way of reading the Bible, though less in vogue today except among remnants of staunch orthodox churches and those who issue encyclicals for birth control—a time-honoured approach to reading Scripture comes looking for its teachings. What christian doctrines are communicated and substantiated by these verses? How does this portion of Scripture contribute to the overall, systematic compendium of biblical truth? Are there any alleged problems with these verses that would subvert one from holding to the articles of faith once for all delivered to the saints?

Going to Numbers 22-24 with such questions in mind leads to a reading something like this:

There is no proof for the Unchangeable Being of God so clear as 23:19.

God is not a man that God would go back on God's word.
God is no son of man that God should repent. . . .

I Samuel 15:29 makes the same affirmation, using practically the same words, when Samuel firmly says "No!" to Saul, God will not take back God's rejecting you as king, even though Saul confessed he had been disobedient in keeping Agag alive from the devastated Amalekites. God's decrees are unchanging; there is no shadow of turning, variableness in God (James 1:17); the LORD cannot do what is contrary to God's everlasting nature (II Timothy 2:13). That is what Balaam is trying to teach Balak who paganly hoped Yahweh could be bought with sacrifices, compelled by magic maybe, controverted by incantations. No, God's determination not to curse but to bless Israel is unalterable, says Balaam, I cannot undo it (23:20); it shall be carried out to your destruction (24:14, 17) almost as inexorably as Moira in a Greek tragedy.

Talk about God's "repenting" something God did (Genesis 6:6; cf. also Amos 7:3,6) is simply an anthropomorphic expression showing the side of mercy in God, the utter grief overwhelming the LORD as the awful punishment, the flood, for example, for ruining the creatures God had made, is readied for execution. But God is divine, unlike men, and never changes God's plans. There is no contradiction in God's telling Balaam, "Do not go!; never curse that folk!, for it is specially blessed" (22:12), and then later, when enemy Balak dogs him with a second delegation and Balaam really hankers for the trip, in saying, almost derisively, "Go ahead then, if you foolishly persist, but not a curse out of you!" (22:20), and still later, in the Angel's stern "Keep on going!, but speak only what the LORD says to you" (22:35). There is no contradiction because God is punishing Moab's evil persistence and Balaam's covetousness by blessing Israel much more and more publicly than if Balak and Balaam had never tried to tempt the LORD. So is the foolishness of God wiser than the cunning of men!, and so does the LORD turn the sin of men into carrying out God's eternal will.

Pendent from the Unchangeable Being of God is the solid truth of the predestined Election of God's people. God swore an oath, says Hebrews 6 (verses 13-18), to Abraham, to make the LORD's immutable counsel doubly confirmed that the descendants of Abraham would be a blessed people, specially tended to (Genesis 22:16-18). And that is exactly the great dogma Numbers 22-24 echoes and reaffirms. "Who can count up the sand grains of Jacob?" (23:10) reveals the very image of God's original promise to Abraham after he separated from Lot (Genesis 13:16). They are "righteous ones" (23:10) not because of what their hands have done, but only because God does not look at their sins (23:21)! Israel is invulnerable because it is God's gracious choice, the LORD's peculiar people. This is what they should remember from the historical incident of Moab king Balak and Balaam, the son of destruction, says Micah 6:5. Jacob was not consumed on the plains of Moab, and the enemies discomfitedly each went their own way (24:25), because the LORD God, who is always the same, the true-to-God's-Word One, elected Israel from eternity (cf. Malachi 3:6).

It follows, therefore, further—because God's elect inhabited a sinful world into which the Son of God had to come (*Cur Deus Homo?*; because God is just and man had sinned, therefore, logically, a God-man was needed to mediate) and because Israel antedated the fulness of time—its royal priesthood could not be completed until the star of Jacob arose, until the Messiah came historically in the flesh. Balaam's fourth prophecy especially foretells unmistakably the coming of Christ (24:17):

A shooting star come from Jacob!
A majestic meteor from Israel is poised aloft

ready to conquer all the enemies of God's elect. This visionary Word is not exhausted by reference to the rule of David or Solomon or Hezekiah or some human king, because there will always be more "Moabites" around, till the end of time when Christ destroys with meteoric fire those who do not know God and who do not obey the Gospel (II Thessalonians 1:6-10). Moses and David are types that prefigure the mediating role, the necessary atonement, the kingship of Christ, but a more patient leader than Moses and a more sinless king than David and one greater than Solomon is needed for the fulfilment of the mercies of unchanging Yahweh to God's elect.

I see him!, but he is not yet there.
I am really seeing him!!, but he is not close enough—

testifies that indeed we prophesy only in part (I Corinthians 13:9). But, though indistinctly seen, the shooting star of Numbers, witnessed to by a wiseman from the East (forerunner of those other wisemen from the East who saw a star! Matthew 2:1-2) before Israel even entered Canaan, is a shining link in the prophetic chain reaching from Genesis 3:15, 12:3, 49:10 all the way to the Apocalypse of John in Revelation 22:16, where Jesus says, "I, Jesus, am the rooting of David and the seed born, the shooting star bright before dawn."

Many other important doctrines of the church are illustrated by what we are told occurred in Numbers 22-24. If so mysterious and unworthy a soothsayer as Mesopotamian Balaam can be a mouthpiece for word-by-word speech of the LORD he probably did not really understand, can there be any question about the nature of organic, plenary inspiration of the Scriptures? Despite their reprobate fears and agitation, the honourable bearing of Balak and his cohorts, and the fact that they sought out a Balaam who had dealings with Yahweh to get "spirit" help, this all indicates the presence of a seed of religion (*semen religionis*) in their minds, although it was smothered by their superstition—which is the factual basis for the doctrine of so-called Common Grace.

But just one more crucial tenet of the church she rightly holds dear, incontrovertibly supported by this passage, should be pointed out: the reality of supernatural miracles—that she-ass saw the angel and spoke (22:23ff). The whole narrative unself-consciously assumes the habit of giving us historical information. Someone who was collecting fables and poems for our edification would not go to the bother of framing them in such geographical accuracy, able to stand up to precise archaeological investigation. There is no hint at all that this balky animal had a premonition of something formidable and terrible, and the heathen soothsayer, so occultly susceptible to animal signs, projected her tremors ventriloquistically into a God speaking, while simultaneously having a vision of an angelic presence. That interpretation is quite contrived. The Bible says matter-of-factly: the ass saw the angel (22:23). . . . God opened the mouth of the ass so she could speak to Balaam (22:28). This is proof that, according to the Scriptures, God, who does not violate natural laws, does at times supercede them temporarily so as to reveal God in a more striking way. We may rest assured that the Bible is infallible to its peripheral details. On matters that surpass human understanding and are not communicated to us—whether the ass spoke Hebrew or Syriac—we will not curiously inquire.

A consistent reading of Numbers 22-24 with concerns like these[4] I would classify as a scholastic, christian orthodox reading.

Critique of Standard Ways of Reading Scripture

My concern so far has been to show that we are not dealing with straw men. The three ways of reading the Bible I have demonstrated are each shaped by a deeply ingrained habit of consciousness. While these varied habits of consciousness are not airtightly exclusive, they do embody quite fundamentally different perspectives on and therefore definite assumptions as to what the Bible is and what it is for. These types of Bible reading, of course, cross denominational lines, and it should be said clearly that each of these approaches—what I have called fundamentalistic, higher-critical, and scholastic—is held by those who profess personally to want to honour Jesus Christ as Lord of their lives and redeeming Creator of the world.

Before I present still an other reading of Numbers 22-24, probing more closely the translated text with which we began, you should understand that my brief critique does not mean to haggle over debatable points so much as to challenge the basic methods employed. What are the hidden a prioris governing each kind of reading and how do these presuppositions focus what they understand to be there? The questions one begins with determine the range and kind of answers that are possible. What can we learn from the results each way of reading comes up with? What are the shortcomings? Does each way miss riches of the Scripture?; methodically mis-take certain points, if not mis-lead fledgling readers who are following that "way"?

Critique of a fundamentalistic reading

The fundamentalistic reading of Numbers 22-24 focuses attention on the vacillating man Balaam, how he was tempted by Balak, and the lesson we should learn from this: how such compromising is evil and punishable by God's judgment.

A fundamentalistic reading of Scripture is interested in the practical lessons we can learn from it. Good about that is that each person is directly faced with the Scriptures as God's command to him or her for one's life, on matters that have life-and-death implications. There is a healthy uncomplicated naiveté about it all, engaging. The Balaam story is relevant. For example, do not accept promotions if it means denying God's people.

Quite wrong about the method, however, despite its laudable intent to serve up inspired instruction for our present-day life, is this: Numbers 22-24 is not about Balaam, Balak, and their doings, except incidentally, and you miss what the holy Scriptures are saying if that is what you take as its meaning. Further, to make Balaam a warning model for the reader is to distort the nature of biblical narrative and ignore the historical solidity of God's disclosure. Scripture never gives biographic snatches to serve as ethical models. Whenever Scripture calls to mind a historical example, it always uses the example to vivify the point it is presently making, not so you can take a lesson from it—the Holy Spirit does not trust even our sanctified homiletic consciences that much.

Thus Luke 17 (verses 31-33) says: In anticipation of Christ's coming, keep Lot's wife in mind; use this world as if you could let it go (cf. I Corinthians 7:31). It does not say: Remember Lot's wife who curiously turned, affectionate still for Sodom, and she got petrified. Don't you covet the sinful city! Flee without turning back while there is still time. . . .

To turn the history of Numbers 22-24 into a parable is to emasculate its revelation.

Besides, making examples out of men or women and deeds in Scripture that we then should follow or abhor—dare to be a Daniel!—is a method with built-in casuistry that breaks the convicting power of the Word of God. Those examples are abstract generalizations, and appeal is made to this individual, that individual, and you, by dint of hard work (not always free from self righteousness), plus God's assistance, of course, to strive to attain that perfection. But because the parallels are not conclusive—Chicago is not Sodom, and I am not Lot's wife; Balaam's invitation from Balak is not remotely within my experience—because my twentieth-century situation and the ancient parallel, abstractly idealized, jibe of sorts only after a dozen qualifications, the binding force is lost, and it has only a moralizing if-you-know-what's-good-for-you type of advice left. It is not: Thus says the LORD to Seerveld . . . .

The value of the fundamentalistic method is that by hook or by crook it gets scriptural words before the consciousness of its hearers, and the worthwhile homilies extracted and forcedly read into passages like Numbers 22-24, depending upon the charisma of the Bible-reading leader, will have wholesome effects upon people's lives. But the shortcut to edification this method proffers is restrictive: the world-upside-down changing messages of Numbers 22-24 is reduced to a mess of moralistic potage. The fundamentalistic method is cheap insofar as it treats God's revelation as a kind of poor christian Richard's Almanac. The Bible is not written to solve my personal problems, but to tell me of the great things God has done. Only so, and then so with a vitality that makes your eyes water, is it true that "All the things written earlier were put in writing for us to understand so that through the firming up and comforting power of the Scriptures we might have hope!" (Romans15:4).

Critique of a higher-critical reading

The scholarly reading of Numbers 22-24 that pieced the oracles and narrative back to two distinct sources, one more prone to theological reflection (Elohist) and an earlier one more story oriented (Yahwist)—this form-critical adaptation of the previous century's evolutionistic fragmentary hypothesis functions superbly in an academic theologian's study, but it does not give a man much to preach from on Sunday to the congregated faithful. This (what I am calling) humanistic mentality corrected that failure somewhat by assuming basically the same literary form-critical analysis of the texts to determine what exactly is there, assuming—subsuming it in service to the leading idea that this sacred writing, whether it be saga or myth or history or whatever at the moment—that, because it is sacred scripture from a more primitive, ancient culture, it must be demythologized, less or more, for us to distil its message relevant for today.

The higher-critical reading of Scripture has a permanent interest in the literary form, a residual concern for the probable origin of the pieces, and above all a drive to get the comparative religious import of the passage existentialized for use in today's sociopolitical world. Good about this method is that it consistently recognizes there is more to the biblical account than private lessons for us as individuals. It is not Balaam and me but Moab and Israel on the docket, and we must discover the secret of this singular folk among the nations to stimulate communal response today. . . .

Very good about the method is its insistence that the reader notice the Bible is there literarily. Bible books, each with their own total character, are composed differently, all made up of longer and shorter units, like Numbers 22:2-24:25 which hangs together as a storied whole, all chock-full of different kinds of stylized features—narrative, songs, conversation, poetic stanzas, genealogical listings, prose of an ordinary diary (in Nehemiah), acrostic verse (like the psalms written so each line begins with the next letter of the Hebrew alphabet [Psalms 9-10, 24, 34, 37, 111, 112, 119, 145]), "sayings" like the four in Balaam's mouth (*maschal* or "saying" usually indicated an epigrammatic nugget of wisdom, like parables). That is, the Bible is written with a large variety of literarily formed wholes, as you expect in literature, and this has a bearing on how you read and understand it. You do not read every portion of the Bible as if it were a chronicle of legislatively adopted proposals and propositions. The Bible is not a monotone citation of texts; it is literature, which demands close, contextual, literary reading.

Also valuable, in a backhanded sort of way, in this approach which emphasizes literary form, composition, and the historical development in getting God's Word inscripturated, is a corrective note against a romanticized concept of inspiration. The Bible was not written by a poet in a garret living on bread and water or by a scribe like Ezra who sat down one night, quill in hand, with half a dozen secretaries, while God dictated stream of consciousness for hours and hours, forty days (cf. the apocryphal book II Esdras 14), which then got published. Rather, David's psalms were occasional, and later sometimes got adapted and used for public, liturgical service (cf. the last two verses added to Psalm 51) for a while, presumably, before they were collected with others. A hundred or so of Solomon's proverbs were transcribed by the community of philosophers at king Hezekiah's court (Proverbs 25:1), a few hundred years later. The Words of Yahweh spoken in judgment against Judah that Baruch wrote down from the mouth of the prophet Jeremiah on a roll got burned by king Jehoiakim—the original biblical scroll was burned!—so God said write it down again and add curses against the king (Jeremiah 36). Luke had knowledge of Mark's account of Christ's doings when God had him put his to writing to certify for Theophilus the reliability of what had been taught orally (Luke 1:1-4). The fourth Gospel selected for reporting only some of what its writer knew about Jesus (John 20:30).

The point is that God's Word got booked all kinds of time-consuming ways, in the moil of human life and blood and language, and the fact that God used copying scribes and editors to get it in script and canon formation is no embarrassment for the holy Scripture's having final authority (any more than that Jesus Christ should blush as less divine because he had an umbilical cord). Important is knowing that the God-breathed specialness of the biblical writings does not make them cabalistic. Instead, when the reader wins a sense of the Scripture's historical timbre, it sharpens his or her listening to the authoritative directive of our Lord that breathes in it, and it will begin to make you keen as a reader to the special appropriateness of various biblical passages.

Quite disconcerting about the method, however, is its covert rationalism, humanism, and touch of skepticism.

I mean this: The good insight that the Bible before us is literature is caught in a highly debatable, dated understanding of literature, typical of early modern western eighteenth-century rationalism and nineteenth-century idealism that frowns upon "grace(s) snatched beyond the reach of" heroic couplets and gives genres fixation power over meaning. But it is not astute to interpret prechristian writings in terms of such literary categories. To say: these repetitious verses look suspicious . . . that tristich ruins the uniformity of its distichous stanza and probably signals corrupt text . . . "Oh, how long" is the way laments begin, so this poem comes out of a dirge situation and has such and such possible meanings . . . benedictions do not describe future events . . . hymns at the most are *vaticinia ex eventu* (postdated "prophecies," after the event happened)—to exegete in this fashion is not to be astute but arbitrarily dependent upon a questionable theory of literature. Repetitious phrases may not be cricket with Jonathan Swift and Diderot, but they are normal fare in ancient Egyptian and Arabian prose and poetry (not to mention medieval ballads, Walt Whitman and contemporary folk song). An extra long poetic line may be inconceivable in Racine or Alexander Pope, but with the little any authority knows about ancient Hebrew metrics today, why must extra poetic feet be corrupt rather than have singular meaning (especially if the Masoretic texts should be followed as religiously as Buber the Jew holds and recent scroll finds show to be confirmed)?

Further, the rationalistic literary critical straitjacket within such Bible reading has consequences much more serious than confining sonnets to love themes and saying elegies must have a melancholy elegance, because the static theory of knowledge to which it is coupled impinges upon the kerygmatic Word of God. To maintain that the third and fourth sayings in Balaam's mouth cannot prophetically promise real entities because they have benedictional form,[5] or to deny historic verity to what a piece relates because it has intensely lyrical, mythopoeic form, not only is atomistically blind to the integral connection of the "oracles" with the whole piece (or Genesis 1 within the whole Pentateuch) but, worst of all, cripples reading the Bible in faith, like a child. Why? First, because it assumes prosaic facts and unreal fiction are the basic epistemological alternatives,[6] and it does not admit how all forms of life action flit through one another and cannot be so academically pigeonholed, and it does not in fact know that there is an untold range of human experience, created reality, and God's doings that are not dreamt of in their two thought constructions. And second, because it absolutizes literary form, so helpful to interpret nuances of meaning in writing, into a tyrannical dictator that restricts, shapes, determines the possible meaning "content" before us, and therefore makes right reading of the Scriptures dependent upon the scientific literary critical judgment of an expert. But God's child, the ordinary Christ-believing man or woman on the street, should not have to wait for the tilting stylistic authorities to determine whether it is this genre or that, how much fact and how much fiction is Jonah's fish story or Jothan's fable of the trees (Judges 9:8-15). God did not present us the Scriptures so that God's child would have to be dependent upon expert human reasoning before one could read its story aright. To make a person's listening to God's written revelation contingent upon a reasoned human norm of interpretation is humanism, the kind I Corinthians spurns (1:18-2:5).

The worst evil still weaseling in this approach to Bible reading, it seems to me, is that it makes the Scriptures a problem. It begs questions like "What actually, historically, came out of Balaam's mouth? Finely phrased blessings as Numbers has it, or round-out curses, which God then turned into blessings, the way Deuteronomy (23:6) and Nehemiah (13:2) report it?" Veteran philological theologians try to solve such problems and second-guess the original documents with a rigour that at best reminds one of Diels-Kranz and D. H. T. Vollenhoven's detective work among the pre-Socratics and at worst seems like the brand of foolish questions and search for origins Paul warned Timothy (I Timothy 1:4) and Titus (3:9) to avoid. These veteran theological problem solvers search for a scientific certainty on matters their own emphasis upon oral tradition makes unsolvable, and the end result is often just sweeping the loose ends under the rug of "editorial revisions."[7] Modern critics have less concern for such sensorial facticity; their skeptical bind is more subtle. A student tried to pin Karl Barth down once by asking, "Did the snake in Genesis 3 actually speak?" Barth's answer, which could be a classic, was, "It's what the snake said that concerns me." What difference does it make whether Balaam's ass literally spoke or not, or things happened *exactly* as it says? Our task, says the humanist critic, is to sift the relevant message from the packing of these striking stories told by great and holy men of God so that the Truth of God breaks through them with a flash into our consciousness and forms us to be men and women of God today—not reportage but kerygma is what we are after!

My point is that, despite extraordinary scholarship, brilliant ripostes, and good intentions (with which hell too is paved), deeply evil here is that the Bible is made intrinsically problematic, the Scriptures themselves are made full of questions for an approaching reader, so that you are not "exactly" sure of things. The reason behind this is the devastating, unexamined presupposition of the method that fallible human response qualifies the writing before us; these Scriptures are documented by wise, holy, Spirit-led men, believable, but human, with the result that the Bible is not so much a canon of God speaking as sanctified writings that serve us as guidelines. Is the account then straightforward? What part of the writing is relevant? A reader must measure it in one's own eyes, with contemporary criteria, for there is no guideline given. This uncertainty, bred by the method, stops a person from "believing *without any doubt* all things contained in" Numbers 22-24, Genesis 1-3, or what have you (my emphasis, *Belgic Confession of Faith*, article 5). To raise such doubt methodically is an evil business, for it puts a stumbling block in front of the faithful, the little ones just beginning to read the Scriptures. For those would-be leaders in Bible reading who occasion such evil the Angel of Yahweh does more than chide with a talking ass: He recommends millstones (Luke 17:2).

Critique of a dogmatic reading

The scholastic reading of Numbers 22-24 found evidence for the Unchangeable Being of God, the eternal Election of God's people, Old Testament messianic prophecies, and support for the doctrine of miracles. Scholastic reading of the Scriptures is always after truths that can be theoretically formulated and held to be universally valid—consistent Bible teaching against all attack.

The strength of that approach is that it realizes a given passage is bigger than the simple incident or thought involved; every verse and portion of Scripture must find its place in the interlocking thought pattern and whole of the Scriptures; there are no isolated instances. This way one is not so apt to misfocus on or reduce the horizons of one's reading to myself and Balaam, or even to Moab and Israel, because somehow Numbers 22-24 must be talking about God and God's plan of salvation. So then you look for it, high and low, under every verb and noun.

The mistake in the method is that it removes the reader half a step from the convicting comfort and humbling which facing God's love and anger brings to a reader; it removes the reader half a step from existential confrontation with the living Word of God and asks him or her to comprehend these realities as codified, propositional dogmas. The provide-ence of the Almighty One, with God's firm decrees, that gives me Grace for eating my daily bread with wife and children, is turned into the Immutable Providence of an Unchangeable Being whose Universal Predestination never slips. The Covenanting One who faithfully keeps calling me back from my sin on pain of death and hears me pray, "Don't take your Holy Spirit away from me!" (Psalm 51:13), is turned into the secret willed decision of God before time began—Election—that has signed, sealed, delivered, and insured certain fortunate ones for life, and unconditionally damned the rest to hell, before time began.[8] That is, the Bible reader is sidetracked from taking what he or she hears to heart into theologizing—systematically distilling and logically coordinating the confessible content of the verses. Theology is vital to an enriched confession, and dogma is a given with educated belief, but when theological dogmatic concerns haunt a person's initial reading, one cannot come listening freshly (part of

Nicodemus's problem). Worse, scholastic theology presumes "the whole counsel of God" means a logical thought pattern, which we can penetrate; it is therefore prone to take off from a scriptural hint and figure out logical implications that must be binding—which gets people believing! caricatures of doctrines like Providence and Election that I just paraphrased. (Doctrine that pulses scripturally is very, very good, but when it is speculative, it is horrid.) The results of scholastic reading are often not so wrong; they are just not right; the light has gone out of the ideas.

Compounding the trouble lodged in this approach is that a precipitate of past doctrines affirmed corporately by the church hardens into a kind of approved *Anschauungsform* (a priori mould for perceiving). A reader who puts on these certified, theologistic glasses is most liable to miss astigmatically the historical, truly temporal, gradually working-out way God deals with humankind, and to stare the development into a schema. Then the reading takes on an overstated, pushy character; for example, on messianic prophecies and types of Christ in the Older Testament (such as Noah, Joseph, Samson, Solomon . . .). There is also a real danger that so long as one reads "out" of the text what fits the mould, it will be approved, whether it is in the text or not. But when you make Scripture a mirror of your dogmatics rather than keep dogmas in their place as two-dimensional reflections of the full-bodied, scriptured Word of God, then you have obstructed genuine Bible reading, coming to the text with the hope that it will playfully wag its tail.[9]

Nobody reads Scripture with a blank mind, and systematic purview is worth much more than a formless haze in your mind or a bent to gather prooftexts which you may later scatter like buckshot upon friend and foe. A christian orthodox reading offers a valuable structure to a person's probing the Scriptures. All the more pity it is that its contribution is ruined by an inordinate fascination with doctrine, whereby the plot of God's revelational history is logicized into a cut-and-dried blueprint, and then absolutized so that you may not see, hear, or read anything contrary to its lines. That is precisely what Hebrews 6 (verses 1-12) warns about: get beyond rehashing the same old foundational doctrines that are as certain as spit—baptism, resurrection of the dead, final judgment—stop practically equating them with Scripture itself, and move on to sanctified social action, or you will stagnate into those who *cannot* repent of their lazy dogmatizing because they have quenched the working of the Holy Spirit. The awful possibility in scholastic Bible reading is that you seem immersed in Bible study but never hear and respond with shock to its news!, getting your human categories fractured, re-formed, charged with action. And if a person or a church is deaf to that power of the Word, which convicts one that doctrine *is* life and life *is* acting commitment—to not hear that Word, yet seem to be busy with it, is a fatal predicament for the person or the church.

A Biblically Reformational* Reading of Numbers 22-24

My intent has not been that now you choose a humanistic existentialistic reading instead of a dead orthodox one, or confirm your preference for Bible reading as institutional Christianity has done it versus the manner of free-lance evangelists who independently build up "their" churches, or that you select a simple heart-warming Gospel conception of the Bible instead of a learned humanistic one that produces lectures from renowned pulpits. All three of these ways of reading the Bible sometimes share the less happy features. The old-fashioned fundamentalist method and the modern higher-critical one (after the scholarly pyrotechnics are executed) hardly differ in that both are interested in what's in it for *me* and my life *now*, although the one gets a conservative individualism from the Bible and the other leans more toward a liberal socialism. Both the traditional orthodox and the fundamentalist reading overlook, if not methodically disavow, the deeply significant world-historical marrow of the biblical account—which the old-style humanist approach secularized as underpinnings to the tales, and doted on, to the exclusion of the singularity of God's acts with Israel.

Neither do I mean to say now comes the perfect way of reading the Bible which supercedes these defective ones. The way of reading Numbers 22-24 I wish to present does not guarantee an infallible understanding of the passage. It does, however,

---

* I have used this term since 1959 to catch several related meanings. "Reformational" identifies (1) a life that would be deeply committed to the scriptural injunction not to be conformed to patterns of this age but to be re-formed by the renewal of our consciousness so that we will be able to discern what God wills for action on earth (cf. Romans 12:1-2); and (2) an approach in history to honour the genius of the Reformation spearheaded by Luther and John Calvin in the sixteenth century, developed by Groen van Prinsterer and Abraham Kuyper in the nineteenth century, as a particular christian tradition out of which one could richly serve the Lord; with (3) a concern that we be communally busy reforming in an ongoing way rather than standing pat in the past tense (*ecclesia reformata semper reformanda est*).

have a certain focus the other ways of Bible reading lack. It is more relaxed too. It listens for the Good News, but in terms of direction rather than maxims; it honours research as an enriching factor, not as a precondition; it acknowledges that the message of the passage is given to be confessed, but then positively instead of apologetically, and fully rather than only in matters of dogma and morals. This other way of reading the Bible is born out of what we call a reformationally christian perspective, and seems to me to do most justice to the riches of the Bible, letting its integrating, compelling, enlightening force work itself out on our whole life in society and God's world.

This reforming approach begins by listening for the specific story at hand, the way mother and dad would read it to you at bedtime, while you keep your ears peaked for literary accents of the piece that carry in-between-the-line overtones and nudge you toward the most significant points of revelation. Then you search out the history-making context of what went on and watch it take shape in the light of the whole Bible. Finally you wrestle yourself to stillness and listen, hear what the Word is telling, overwhelming you, of God's marvelous dealings with humankind in God's creation, headed for glorious completion.

Telling the true story

God was bringing God's people freed, up out of Egyptland, and everybody and his brother in the Near East knew about it. We heard how Yahweh dried up the waters of the Red Sea for you!, Rahab told Joshua's two spies; and she continues: I know Yahweh your God, who is God in the heavens and on the earth, Yahweh has given you the land—every inhabitant is shaking with fear! (Joshua 2:9-11). Possessed by *Angst*, irrational fear, like Europeans before the advancing Russian armies of world war II, Moab dreaded the uncounted mass of Israelites camped on the plains at her doorstep. There was something uncanny, supernatural, existence-threatening about this special folk with an Almighty God—*total* victory over the Amorites and Og. Weaponry you could touch would not be strong enough for preserving Moab land, life, and possessions. Demonic powers would be needed, aid from the spirit world, an effective curse to break the spell of these Hebraic invaders from the wilderness.

So the pastoral, settled people of Moab, under generalissimo Balak, with the nomadic traders of Midian, whose sheikhs had sold Joseph into Egypt years and years ago and who frequented Mesopotamia, where Laban had lived to whom Jacob fled, where Balaam now resided—these cunning, fearful leaders tried to engage the famed barû-priest of the Near East (a kind of military medicine man), whose sorcery was the best to be had; in fact, he could have visitations at night from Yahweh self! They promised Balaam, with almost satanic earnestness, the summit of worldly glory (22:17; 24:11). Tickled in his pride by this ceremonious call upon his prestigious powers, Balaam wanted to go, try his hand at making history. God's telling him Israel is a specially blessed people did not register in his wilfulness. God let him go, so that the masterful rule of the LORD upon *all* nations of the world would be revealed and proclaimed, already in the day of Moses, with unusual clarity.

Balaam went, but Yahweh stopped the Canterbury Tales jollity in his trip by the speech of his dumb ass and by appearing self as obstructing, righteous Angel with sword in hand. This is no lark, said the LORD: Israel brings those who confront her to the edge of life or death! Marshaling the powers of darkness to frustrate my faithful purpose to bring the sons of Jacob into Canaan is an evil business worthy of death! Do you want to die, Balaam? Speak only what I shall put in your mouth.

That is precisely what happened, though Balaam half-heartedly joined Balak in fussing religiously through the tedious work of pagan sacrifices. Then God opened the mouth of Balaam, like an ass, and he spoke out unutterable blessings upon the people of God: (1) How wonderfully secure, separated by God from the rest of the world, you have been in the past! How like sands of the seashore you are becoming. . . . (2) The LORD *is* bringing you up out of Egyptland, because God said God would, looking past your sins, telling you in the LORD's time what is in store. So celebrate, indeed! Yahweh your king is leading you on to victory! (3) The LORD God shall establish you on the earth with paradise gardens, plenty, and a king. You are a holy people! Who blesses you will be blessed, and who curses you shall be cursed!

After Balak, in anger, forgot his royal manners and told Balaam to beat it, God opened the mouth once more and he foretold (4) the coming of One who would make Israel more than conqueror, Someone with shining, meteoric proportions compared to their years of wilderness wandering and poised uncertainty before entering enemy Canaan. Amid wars and rumours of war till the end of time, certain it is, however, that in the strength of this shooting star God's people shall overcome! Then Balak and Balaam separated.

The aftermath (told in Numbers 25 and 31:1-20) shows the spite of a public figure who did not get the honour he coveted. Balaam went to the Midianite elders and told them how to corrupt Israel, break the LORD'S favour upon them. And it succeeded insofar that 23-24,000 Israelites were killed by the plague Yahweh sent to punish them for wooing, sleeping, fertility-worshiping with the Midianite and Moabite young women, who were systematically sent to beguile the sons of Jacob in the shadows of the cliffs of Peor, the holy hill places of Baal, from where Balaam had spoken the blessings upon them of their jealous God Yahweh. Not till Phinehas, Aaron's grandson, speared an Israelite boy and Midianite girl through the bellies as they lay together did the LORD's anger toward Israel soften. Then God commanded Moses to spoil and annihilate the Midianites. While doing this, they caught Balaam in the company of the Midianite chiefs, judged, and executed him for his evil designs.[10] Purified once more, Israel waited for the leading of the LORD.

Discerning literary contours

This history, including "the dumb ass speaking with human voice," as II Peter 2:16 recounts it, is presented with a disarming, matter-of-fact freshness, yet withal piercingly imaginative depiction of the conflicts above and below the surface of the personages. God's face got red with indignation at the perky obstinacy of Balaam on his way, says the Scriptures (22:22). Later, Balaam's face flushed red with indignation at the obstinacy of his ass (22:27); and still later, Balak's face got red with indignation at Balaam's obstinate blessings (24:10). They all got red in the face! This light artistic touch points up in passing how God recompenses the sin of men in kind. And there is the penetrating subtlety of reporting conversations: Do not go with the men because Israel is not to be cursed, God told Balaam (22:12). Yahweh will not let me go, Balaam told the envoys, omitting the crucial reason (22:13). Balaam would not come with us, the envoys told Balak (22:14). The sloughing-off twist to God's initial Word suggests how unintelligible God's revelation is to those bent on evil. It took a while too for Balak to get through his heathen, sacrificing head of *do ut des* ("I give so that you give"—the religious bargaining of pagandom) the idea that he was dealing not with a buyable man but with the God of heaven and earth; not till the first actual blessing shook him up did he ask Balaam before the second ordeal, "What did *Yahweh* speak?" (23:17).

The whole telling of this history has the temper of excitement, the unusual, crisis, and climax. Something truly serious must be at stake for God to show up personally as the Angel of Yahweh to threaten this foreign soothsayer Balaam into obedience. And when an ass, a beast of burden, shames a man made to image God!, you have something awful, apocalyptic on your hands, like the moon turning blood red, and not some kind of Shakespearian comic relief. The forces of heaven and hell, damning curses that kill and blessing, talking animal and stinking sacrifices, seventy times seven, are converging on the plains of Moab where the mighty of the earth wait in dread. There is a showdown coming. The "sayings" have the elevated language great men use before they die (cf. II Samuel 23:1-7); poetry and phrases like "So speaks the big man whose eye was shut" are not pompous but sublime, fit for the occasion. There is an end to something coming up, and will there be a beginning? The creation, flood . . . the calling of Abraham and giving him in his faith the promises at the time of Job, Isaac, Jacob, Joseph, and Judah, exodus from Egypt, covenanting at Sinai, and a generation's wandering through the cruel desert watching the old ones die off—it has all come to an end now in the plains of Moab. Will the LORD God Yahweh fulfil God's promise to bring the children of Abraham, Isaac, and Jacob into a land where they shall dwell together, God and folk, as lovers at rest?

That is the time when Satan does his worst: if Satan can only stymie God's unfolding God's glory at this stage of development! At every critical point in history the devil goes dragon to swallow up the child about to be born to the woman of Revelation 12. This is what is going on in Numbers 22-24! That is why the Balaam-Balak episode is quoted throughout the Bible as a terribly significant event: the LORD delivered Israel from the Evil One! Yahweh remained the Almighty Faithful One to God's people! Joshua lists it in the same breath with the ten plagues of Egypt during his final exhortation to the people to continue serving the LORD (Joshua 24:9-10); and the prophet Micah cites it as the most conclusive evidence in Yahweh's lawsuit with Judah (Micah 6:5), at about the time when Assyria was hauling off the covenant-breaking ten tribes of Israel to captivity, scattering them forever to the wind. God remained true when the chips were down, overwhelmingly so!, is the initial message of Numbers 22-24. And Israel?

Detecting the history-making context

You can almost hear the LORD cry in Hosea 9:10 as God tells the prosperous debauched citizens of the northern kingdom:

> *I found Israel in the wilderness to be like lush grapes.*
> *Like the most succulent, the freshest early figs on a fig tree*
> *—that's how I experienced your (desert) fathers.*
> *But they!—they crawled over to the Baal of Peor!*
> *They went in and sucked on that shameful thing!*
> *They became as rotten as what they were loving. . . .*

With that the whole historical panorama opens up around Numbers 22-24. The virginity of Israel was ruined in the plains of Moab despite the protecting faithfulness of her Covenanting God. That damned Balaam, stopped from cursing, still connived to get the sons of Israel to break their married vows to Yahweh. And an era ended.

No more Moses mediating the wrath of Yahweh alone in the desert. No more honeymooning in the wilderness—that's what it was for God. Serving up breakfast of manna in bed every morning . . . dallying with God's people far away from everyone else. The Israelite often saw only the sweltering heat, the inconvenience of lack of water; they murmured and bitched, revolted and dragged their feet, but at least "they had no strange god at all with them" then, says the Song of Moses (Deuteronomy 32:12). And Yahweh was happy as a bridegroom, tasting the sweet fruits of his beloved (Jeremiah 2:2). God was freeing them from bondage!, from being slaves in Egypt. God was giving Israel the Law!, a gift to free them from death and dead ends, and to set them firmly on the way of life. The LORD was protecting her like the hair of her head, like a wild ox against the chariots of mighty pharaoh (23:22; 24:8), against the treacherous Amalekites and their dynasty of Agags (Exodus 17:8-13), against crippling disease and snakes that strike while the sun shines.

> *The LORD surrounded God's people carefully, gave them attention, protected them as if they were God's own skin.*
> *Like a huge eagle that rustles out its nest and hovers over the young birds,*
> *So the LORD stretched out his wing, caught his (fledgling) people, and bore them aloft on his wide open pinions.*
> *(Deuteronomy 32:10-11)*

God who hates sin was being faithful to God's promises in the wilderness, a bouquet of promises with a history. It had been vowed to faithful Abraham that he would have a multitude of believing children in whom *all kinds* of blooded people would be blessed (Genesis 12:3; repeated to Jacob at Bethel, Genesis

28:14). It had been promised to Abraham that his believing descendants would inherit Canaan from the LORD (Genesis 17:8; repeated to Jacob, Genesis 28:13). This is what Yahweh was bringing to pass under Moses: sifting the children of Israel till those with faith remained, and chaff like Korah, Dathan, and Abiram, and those who would have remained in Egypt, fell through the sieve, dead. To get into Canaan took faith. You could not enter the land of milk and honey just because you could fight (cf. Numbers 14:40-45). God had made that clear to the Israelites soon after they left Egypt, extending and updating for a whole people the blessings covenanted with the patriarch of old:

> *If you will really listen, pay attention to my voice,*
> *If you keep, hold tight my covenant vowed [with you],*
> *Then you will be something special belonging to me*
> *compared to all other folk*
> *(the whole earth, of course, belongs to me):*
> *you will become a ruling order of anointed ones,*
> *a holy people. . . . (Exodus 19:5-6)*

So honeymooning and winnowing to holiness, God brought God's people up to the last obstacle: king Balak, the princes of Moab, Midian, and Balaam the destroyer. And what does God do for God's people in the plains of Moab? Reaffirm the vows!, sing the old love songs that are still new because the love has not grown cold:

> *You are special, compared to all other peoples of the world. (23:9)*
> *Your sins and blemishes are covered before my eyes (23:21)—I love you.*
> *Whoever blesses you will be blessed, and whoever tries to curse you shall be cursed. (24:9)*

An exact repetition of what was told Abraham (Genesis 12:3), but now ominously intensified with meaning because God has Balaam heap it like coals of fire upon the heads of Israel's sworn enemies, who are trying to curse!

Moab, conjoined by Midian, and nearby Edom—all, like Esau, fiercely hated Israel because it was specially favoured, blessed, covenantedly anointed to be a holy race. Could they but bruise Jacob's heel, they would be glad. So their present will to curse came out of a lasting enmity against God's will to bless; and the enmity was well known. Long before, in his victory doxology at the Red Sea, Moses had singled out the apostate descendants of Lot and Esau and "all the sons of Seth," foretelling their paralytic fear at the coming of God's people (Exodus 15:15). Soon after the present encounter, Moses decreed, and hundreds of years later governor Nehemiah, who began reading Moses again to the citizenry of rebuilt Jerusalem, decreed that no Moabite (or Ammonite) could stay mixed in with the congregated faithful of God because they had hired Balaam and his wiles to break the bond of blessing Jacob enjoyed with the Covenanting LORD (Deuteronomy 23:4 7; Nehemiah 13:1-3). The final apocalyptic Word is also given right here in the fourth and last visionary "saying" from Balaam's mouth: Moab and Edom, along with Amalek and all violent men of vanity, are marked for dispossession and destruction under the shooting star to come from Jacob (24:17-18, 20). Not till "Shiloh come" in the last days will these disgruntled antagonists of the blessing upon Jacob, upon the lion Judah (cf. Genesis 49:9-10), and therefore antagonists of Yahweh, not till then will they be finally stopped.[11] But in the meantime Israel remains a specially blessed people (22:12).

That Israel is specially blessed carries over at this historical turning point and continues to dominate everything that can happen to her, even Balaam's making her for the first time into a whore. Now there will be no more Moses and honeymooning in the wilderness. Now is the time for Joshua, judges, and kings, life in Canaan, widespread infidelity, empire grandeur, temple instead of tabernacle, and heartbreak for the LORD. But always—a specially blessed people of God! It is almost unbelievable how Yahweh picks up the pieces God's faithless bride makes of God's handiwork, and even enlarges the horizons within which the LORD still holds her hand. The office of focusing God's promises for the people Abraham and Moses bore is to be carried on now by the house of David. Israel's heavenly king Yahweh, who lives right among them (23:21), will raise up a king in Israel!, who shall extend the majestic rule of the LORD over the face of the earth (24:7). Prophets too will be provided by the LORD for the good of God's people. You can almost sense it from the performance of the stranger Balaam, especially when he says: there is no black magic or witchery in Jacob trying to manipulate unseen powers or ferret out secrets of the universe; God simply tells them, when it is time, what marvelous things God has been doing lately and wants them to do (23:23). As the Israelites settle down, develop a culture, face tasks more differentiated than honeymooners face, it will take a large band of specially cultivated, anointed men and women to make God's will known to all the people.

And God's people now must rule! That is truly a critical change in the offing for God's wilderness-wandering people. No longer will they be a folk securely off to the side, alone with the LORD (23:9). The new order is to rule, secure in the meteoric power of their God, establish God's rule *historically* right among the nations (24:7, 17-18). Sometimes that "Rule" will mean incorporating other-blooded strangers who believe, like Rahab and Ruth, into the company of God's people (till the faith of Cornelius, the New Testament Italian centurion, makes the reach of God's original promise to Abraham unmistakably evident; cf. Acts 10:1-11:18, especially verses 28 and 34-35 of chapter 10). "Rule" may also mean fight to the death, as the sons of Israel had to do when the Amalekite enemy Haman (son of Hammedatha the Agag-ite!; Esther 3:10; 8:3) balled together the political power of Persia to exterminate the Jewish nation (Esther 3:8-11; 9:24). But "Rule" shall always mean conquering God's enemies, those who hate God's covenanting jealousy and will not exercise the LORD's way; "Rule" always means "possessing" such cursing people, subjecting them and their ways to the peace, the rich fulness, Shalom!, that comes with bearing fruit obedient to the Will of Yahweh. The "Rule" of Jacob's shooting star demolishes nations of the world or is a blessing to them. And those within the city of God, concludes the fourth "saying," who desert it, shall be ruined (24:19); those who stay and respond with service to the LORD shall catch on to a life with blessed people and die the death of the righteous.[12]

the preaching of the gospel of Christ, especially in the manner of the early church

Listening to and hearing the kerygmatic message

There is much more going on in our surroundings than we are aware of. Angels, God's gift, are busy tending to the delicate balance of various lives that look composed in public, warding off evil, pulling out of danger, strengthening for an ordeal (Psalm 34:8). As Elisha's servant could not see the fiery chariots and horses stacked on the mountain of Dothan, outnumbering the Syrian hosts (II Kings 6:13-17), so our faith is usually too inexperienced, our vision so dim—we are too filled with our own musings, preoccupied with gigantic Self-endeavours—that we hardly ever see even a stray angel or two within ten feet of our path, and we would want to feel at least his biceps before we would admit he was more than a paper angel, a dogmatic one. But blessed are those who not seeing believe, experience the forces of heaven mysteriously attending their earthly doings. The presence of God is real! God's Spirit is in our gatherings; and Christ with an army of angels—merciful obstructionists!—is within our call—not the demented request of disbelief to test God, but within reach of a thankful plea for help. Part of the Good News of Numbers 22-24 is that, thank God!, Yahweh Sabbaoth guards God's people, unknown to them, from the tireless conspiring of evil ones, like the Angel of Yahweh and his company protected Israel, unawares, in the plains of Moab from their adversaries' cunning. (The LORD guards even those just lodging with God's people, like the non-Hebraic Kenites of 24:21-22; cf. Numbers 10:29-32 and Judges 1:16.) Satan knows what he is up against and tries to pervert with unbelief our being secure (cf. Luke 4: 9-12). But Yahweh has God's loved ones under continuous, mighty guard.

God shall not let your foot stumble and fall.
The One who cares for you does not tire asleep.
Do you hear! God never gets drowsy;
The One who is taking care of Israel never falls asleep.
The LORD Yahweh is the One who cares for you too.
The LORD Yahweh is that shade wholly covering you on your right side (so that) the sun does not strike you with sunstroke during the day nor the moon wilder you in the night.
The LORD Yahweh is truly taking care of you, keeping you from all evil.
The LORD is watching out for your life.
The LORD Yahweh is taking care of your every coming and going,
And God will do it from now on and for ever more.
(*Psalm 121:3 -8*)

Thank God there is so much angelically going on, and we do not have to bother our heads figuring it out, except to know, that is, live knowing what Elisha told his servant boy: don't be afraid, there are thousands more with us who believe than with the others.

There are probably not many virgins reading this booklet, those who never had or took a lover, or have not been sullied by the pimp of modern advertising. I doubt whether there are any chaste people either, who have known, slept, given themselves bodily, from the crown of their head to the tips of their stretched-out bare toes, only to One, always and forever. We all go whoring, after our fashion. No Christian who once publicly pledged love to Jesus Christ, incarnation of the jealous Yahweh, perhaps as a gawky teenager, sincere as pimples—no Christian, no matter how respectable looking, has been true as a lover to the Ruler of heaven and earth. Each one has his or her secret love kept at the expense of the LORD's Rule, a deeply intimate desire, dulness, ambition, or peeve that we polish covetously only for ourselves and will not throw away into the refiner's fire. Such double loving does not bother us much because it seems to be minor, and our bridegroom is gone for the moment. . . .

But part-time whoring—any Christian who denies he or she does it is a liar, says the Scriptures (I John 1:8, 10)—part-time whoring breaks the power of God's people. Christ's disciples could not cure a disturbed man because of their meagre faith (*oligopistia*), their not-thoroughly-exercised faith, to the point of urgent supplication and fasting (Matthew 17:14-21). It is so that the LORD uses among God's people those who pledge less than wholehearted, impassioned love (*agapé*); at least he once received Peter's expressed devotion that was no more than par for ordinary affairs (*philia*)—but only because Peter was grieved and humbled by Jesus' understanding the broken-down ordinariness of his commitment (John 21:17)! God will use—stunning wonder!—us part-time whores who believe, whom God's Son wedded, welded to himself, to establish his rule, *if* we are shamed by this confession, *if* we detest the fact that our coveted duplicity breaks the power of bringing his blessing to the world, *if*, that is, we are waiting helplessly to be brought under the comforting, convicting power and direction of His Word. There is no chance, however, of our hearing what the Spirit is saying to the churches in Numbers 22-24 if we are not speechlessly ashamed of ourselves before God's face.

The Word of God in this Old Testament passage, contextually set within chapters 20-21 and 25, says two things:

First: You are called to be a community specially separated, anointed by God to carry out the blessing of Yahweh's Rule among the nations of the world.

A lot of time has gone over the historical dam since God opened Balaam's mouth to speak his "sayings" and had them recorded in Scripture to build us up wise in the faith (II Timothy 3:14-17). Moabites, Midianites, Amalekites, and twelve tribes of Israel have mutated into alignments of Arab and Jew, Buddhist and Christian, western humanist and oriental peoples of the world. In fact, Israel of Moab's plains has become today what

Esau's Edom was then: naturally first, the trunk, the one you would expect to inherit the choicest blessings, advantaged by having had the words of God entrusted to them (Romans 3:1-2), but, instead, largely pruned out of the family of God because they rejected Jesus Christ as the Messiah and trusted in their own good works. Now, anybody captivated by that rejected Jesus as Lord, who by faith gets grafted like wild olive shoots into the tree of Life, says Paul to the Romans, inherits the gifts and calling of God's people (cf. Romans 9-11, especially 9:30-32 and 11:11, 28-32).

> *Look! a folk that settles itself securely off to the side,*
> *and does not reckon itself as just*
> *one of the peoples of the world (23:9). . . .*
> *A majestic meteor from Israel is poised aloft . . .*
> *It is Israel that is gaining productive power! (24:1 7-18)*

God's people are marked by being set apart, not one of the majority, peculiarized by their not adopting the "shape," the pattern, the fashion of their age because the Word of God is forming their communal consciousness to work out historical formations that bend the mind to see God rather than men (Romans 12:1-2). The throng of God's people culled from every race and tongue by the Holy Spirit is always strangely at odds with its contemporaries who believe otherwise, because God's people take their orders from God's revelation as the Truth and confess other sources of direction are spurious!, and that offends people, sounds rather "holier than thou" coming from an association of part-time whores. The fact that God's people do not keep their distinctive "sanctity" to themselves either, but feel compelled to be breaking down arguments and every obstacle raised up against the simple knowledge of God, bringing *every* thought, every sensation even!, every social relation and institutionalized fabric away captive, in the subjection of this Messiah (II Corinthians 10:5; Philippians 1:9-11)—whether it be hacking down idolatry in Canaan BC, refusing the food of "neutral" labouring guilds in Asia

Minor AD, or requesting christian schooling in North America today—that is an affront to those who live out of a more tolerantly human dynamic, it smacks of an Old Testament exclusivism.

But the New Testament backs up Numbers literally:

> *Jesus Christ gave himself for us so that He might free us from every kind of lawlessness and might clean us up as the specially-belonging-to-him people, fanatic at deeds working good. (Titus 2:14)*
>
> *Christ made us a ruling order, ones anointed for God his father. . . . (Revelation 1:6)*
>
> *You are a selected sort: a ruling priesthood, a separated folk, a people in trusteeship, so that you may compellingly broadcast the glories of the One who called you out of the dark into the wonderment of his enlightenment. (I Peter 2:9)*

That is the calling to be heard in the "sayings" of Numbers 22-24: become a sanctified, specially-belonging-to-him people, an irrefragable community exercising the LORD's Rule upon the earth, worthy of God's name. This calling is proclaimed!—it is not just listed as a vocational option—proclaimed as *defining* believers in the LORD. We had better face what that means, because the honeymoon of Christianity in history is past. The more acute have seen that the "established church" has been found wanting by the world (maybe by God too) and will no longer be tolerated unless churchmen auction off their candlesticks to put in neon lights, so to speak, adding another "Y" to do good in the community. But if God's people begin to act together biblically *as God's people*, even outside the church doors, responding to the full-orbed concretion of this "priestly ruling" call of the Scriptures, turning sacred cows of the democratic way of death upside down (cf. Acts 17:6), then there is going to be persecution. God's people who respond to the apocalyptic "sayings" of Numbers 22-24 in faith are going to get hurt, especially when the secular mind sees that God's people experience this proclaimed calling, proclamation!, as a blessing, like a fiery cloud showing the way, sealing them from all evil, making them unafraid. Such Grace-given abandon and security that comes with obedience to the LORD infuriates those who do not serve our God. What happens then shall sadly confirm the fact that the temper of Numbers 22-24 is quite close to that of Isaiah 24-27, Matthew 24-25, and the Apocalypse of John.

Second: Shun, rid your communion of its modern-day Balaams, for they are destroying the people of God.

This heavy, terrible Word is explicit in the New Testament. Jude ranges Balaam in a row with Cain and the revolutionary Korah (verse 11). Revelation 2 (verses 14-15) identifies Balaam teaching with the circulating ideas and practices of the Nicolaitans.[13] II Peter, warning against pseudoprophets and deceptive teachers, says: after leaving the right path, they wandered around and now have snuggled into the way of Balaam . . . who loved the satisfaction of not being straight (2:15). Peter, Jude, and John show the true story of Balaam and Balak in its significance for God's people after Christ's resurrection: the worst evil the people of God can suffer is to have Balaam-like leaders who talk out of two sides of their mouth—

We are for christian things and the great promises of God,	*but beware of separatistic zealotry: there are an awful lot of things we have in common with the unbeliever.*
Of course, obey the commands of God,	*but there are so many things the Bible says neither Yes nor No to—you are free there!; there's no law!; there's a lot of latitude for private decision . . . you can mix with unbelievers, partake of their*

society so long as . . . you give God what belongs to God, as specified.

Killers!, says Scripture. Dirty, double-crossing, damnable killers of God's people!

The Scriptures have authority, but your interpretation of the Scriptures is not infallible, and they don't cover everything.

This is Balaam teaching, the practice of Nicolaitans, says the New Testament, and God damns it to hell.

Give your hand to God; also join hands with adiaphora —not evil things!, of course —adiaphora, things that are neither here nor there religiously, that are not clear, about which there can be dispute (like Peter and Paul even had), matters of historical determination, of human opinion. . . .

Nicolaitans raised this double-handed practice into *policy*, made it, obviously or not, the leading *principle of operation* in life, recommending it, with the enormously polite learning, cavils, and striking modifications that are the trademark of latitudinarians, recommending it especially to the young. Killers!, say the Scriptures, who insinuate what is really a pattern of promiscuity, baiting those who cannot yet stand on their own feet (II Peter 2:14).

> *To the elderly authorities at Pergamum write: "Stop it cold and change it!, or I myself shall come in a flash to fight with the followers of Balaam with the cutting sword of my spoken Word." (Revelation 2:14-17)*

To the elderly authorities at Thyatira write, says Christ: "Get rid of those urbane seducers or I will root you with them and their children out of my body!" (Revelation 2:20-23)

Pray God that the modern-day Balaams be blinded, that their counsel be confounded, that they be struck dumb as asses!, because in our day, says the gospel according to Mark (13:22), Balaam figures shall mislead even the elect, if it's possible. . . . [14]

What rest remains for the people of God (Hebrews 4:9)? It is not far away or hidden, way up in heaven or overseas, but as close as Numbers 22-24 in the mouth and heart of a believer.

Speak the simple prophetic Word of God against the two-mouthed, two-handed Balaam policy, and be driven by the principle of "search the Scriptures till your eyes go open, knowing what God's Will is on those matters that seem indiscernible."
Work and pray, not alone, but as a specially consecrated community in the wide world of God, pray: "Our Father . . . your Rule come on earth as it is being done by the angels; establish the work of our believing, weak hands."

This Word of Numbers 22-24 is what gives restfulness to God's people. Those who obey are already blessed, protectively covered by the wing of the LORD. That should make any faint-hearted observers jealous, wanting to hear Numbers 22-24 too, believing what it says. Then the concluding blessing of Numbers 6 (verses 24-26) is also for your listening ears:

May the LORD God bless you.
May God keep you safe.
May the LORD God turn God's friendly face toward you,
and be gracious to you.
May the LORD God give you God's smile of love,
and present you with Shalom.
Shalom!

Notes

1 This prototype presentation is collated, paraphrased, extrapolated from sources like the following: Baptist Alexander Maclaren, *Expositions of Holy Scripture* (Grand Rapids: Wm. B. Eerdmans, 1959), I, 367-376; Baptist W. B. Riley, "Kadesh To Canaan" in *The Bible of the Expositor and the Evangelist* (Cleveland: Union Gospel Press, 1926), III, 99-109; Presbyterian Clarence Edward Macartney, "Balaam—the man who reached for two worlds and lost both" in *Sermons on Old Testament Heroes* (Nashville: Abingdon Press, 1935), pp. 196-207; Congregationalist Joseph Parker, "Balaam . . . " in *The People's Bible. Discourses upon Holy Scripture* (New York: Funk and Wagnalls, 1886), III 302-339; Bishop Joseph Butler, "Upon the character of Balaam" in *Sermons* (New York: Robert Carter, 1844), pp. 82-92; and Matthew Henry, *The Comprehensive Commentary on the Holy Bible* (Boston: Shattuck & Company, 1835), pp. 514-526.

An interesting mistake Butler made in what Maclaren calls "Bishop Butler's great sermon" on Balaam is that Butler supposed one of the most pregnant passages of the prophet Micah (6:8) to be a direct quote of Balaam! in answer to Micah 6:6-7 which Butler misunderstood to be reporting a question of Balak (cf. 6:5). Quite a few "divines" followed the learned bishop's mistake; Samuel Cox says Cardinal Newman, scholar Ewald, as well as he himself and others shared this opinion.

But Balaam did not speak Micah 6:8, so there is no headache to make it "rhyme" with all the other scriptural references which unanimously seem to judge Balaam as evil minded.

2 Sigmund Mowinckel's breakdown of the section (see "Der Ursprung der Bileamsage," ZAW, 48:233-271 [1930]) illustrates the form-critical methods in its modification of Wellhausen's earlier popularized developmental, fragmentary-sources hypothesis. J = Yahwist narrative, E = later Elohist slant, RJE = editorial touches connecting JE.

J	22:2-3a, 5*ab*, 6*b*, 6*ab*, 7*a*	**E**	22:3b-5a*a* b*a*, 6a*a* b
	22:22-34 (ass-angel of Yahweh)		22:7b-21 (Balaam-Balak)
	22:37, 39		22:36, 38, 40
	23:28		22:41-23:25 (26?) (oracles I & II)
	24:2-11, 14-19 (oracles III & IV) (24:25)		(24:25)

RJE	22:35
	23:27
	23:29-24:1
	24:12-13 (late) 24:20-24

3 This mock-up model reading is the edited fusion of the following sources into

which documents it could be reconstructed: (M) Sigmund Mowinckel, "Der Ursprung der Bileamsage"; (R) Wilhelm Rudolph, *Der "Elohist" von Exodus bis Josua* (Berlin: Alfred Töpelmann, 1938), pp. 97-128; (G^1) G. B. Gray, "Moab and Israel," ICC on Numbers, pp. 307-379; (G^2) Herman Gunkel, *What Remains of the Old Testament and other essays*, trans. A. K. Dallas, preface by James Moffat (New York: Macmillan Co., 1928), 186 pp.

Among other works consulted were: W.F. Albright, "The Oracles of Balaam," *JBL*, 63:207-233 (September 1944); Samuel Cox, *Balaam* (London: Kegan Paul, Trench & Co., 1884) 208 pp.; Walter Lock, "Balaam," *JTS*, 2:161-173 (January 1901).

4 Certain ideas for this reading specimen were sprung from: E.W. Hengstenberg, *The History of Balaam and his Prophecies*, trans. J.E. Ryland, bound with "Dissertations of the Genuineness of Daniel and the Integrity of Zechariah" (Edinburg: T. & T. Clark, 1848), pp. 331-561; John Calvin, Numbers 22-24 in *Commentarii in quatuor reliquos Mosis libros in formam harmoniae* (Amsterdam: J.J. Schipper, 1671), 1:659-671.

5 Cf. Mowinckel ("Der Ursprung der Bileamsage," p. 248): "Das zweite Lied hat noch deutlicher die Form einer Weissagung von konkreten Ereignissen. Der 'Stern' und die 'Sternrute' (der Komet), der aus Jaekob steigt and hervorstrahlt und die Schläfen Mo'abs (der Schet-Söhne) zerschmettert und sich Edom (Seeir) zum Eigentum macht, ist weder Messias noch irgend welche wirklich zukünftige Grösse—*das ist einfach mit der Erkenntnis der Eigenart der literarischen Gattung solcher Lieder gegeben*, die sich überhaupt nur mit dem beschäftigen, was schon Wirklichkeit geworden ist—sondern David, der Mo'ab und Edom bezwang und unter Israel legte" [my emphasis].

6 Gray exhibits a positivistically normed historiography and opinion that poetry is contrary to established fact in discussing Numbers 22:41ss. "Now the mere events would have crowded a single day unduly; but when it is considered that the solemn sacrifices were offered on three different sites (not immediately contiguous, and, according to some identifications, separated from one another by more than a day's journey), it will be seen that we are here moving (as, *e.g.*, in Job 1:13-22) in the realm of poetry, not of fact. . . . Once this is appreciated we may also dismiss the question how the king of Moab and his princes ventured unprotected into the territory N. of the Arnon, though it had just been captured by the Israelites from the Amorites. The unreality or, in other words, the poetical character of the narrative extends apparently to the source E. It is less obvious that the reasons stated apply to the source J" (*op. cit.*, p. 341).

7 Mowinckel assigns 22:7b-21 to Elohist tradition, and then expurgates every reference to Yahweh (22:13, 18, 19)—what does not fit his assumption—expurgates it from the text as redactional filling (*op. cit.*, p. 234 n. 1). He presumes

reference to "official ambassador" is E and to "grey-haired elders" is J, yet he faults Von Gall for using the different verbs for "cursing" (*'arar* and *kabab*) to distinguish sources similarly. Rudolph too takes Von Gall to task for "die minutiöse Quellenscheidung"—"in der Tat ist ein Redaktor, der mit Schere und Kleistertopf arbeitet und aus Versfetzen Mosaiken legt, unvorstellbar" (Rudolph, *op. cit.*, p. 107). But granted excesses exist and could be reduced *ab absurdum*: what supports each man's contradicting selection of criteria except an *ipse dixit*?

8 With remarkably felt precision, void of scholastic speculation, Calvin comments on Numbers 23:19: sed in consideranda ejus natura meminerimus nullis conversionibus obnoxium esse, quoniam superat omnes caelos. . . . quia Deus in suis decretis firmus sit (in considering God's nature we should remember that God is not liable to any turn-arounds, because God is above all heavens . . . because God in God's decrees holds firm). His summation of the whole three chapter episode too is a model of concrete warmth and Bible-integrating wisdom (ad 24:24-25): Summa ergo est, turpiter abiise populi electi hostes re infecta: quoniam Deus eos dissipavit (The import of it all then is this: the enemies of God's chosen people fled in disarray, without having accomplished their purpose, because God routed them). Calvin is seldom as bookish as subsequent Calvin*ists* are made out to be.

9 In showing how static, explained, *finita* the thought world of scholastic Rome is compared to a genuinely Reformed (*reformanda*) habit of thought, Okke Jager quotes a petition from Dutch poet Greshoff to Our Father:

> *Geef ons een teken: laat de Grote Beer*
> *Zo nu en dan eens kwispelstaarten, Heer!*
>
> *Give us a sign: Let the Big Dipper*
> *Now and then wag its tail, Oh Lord!*

10 Perhaps that is when Balaam, in his defence, recounted what had transpired unknown to the Israelites beforetime, and Moses wrote it down in the journal God had him keeping of the wilderness events; cf. Numbers 33:2. Another possibility is that what took place according to Numbers 22-24 was first recorded in the book "Wars of Yahweh" (quoted in Numbers 21:14-15), which dealt with the seizure of Canaan, especially the East-of-Jordan lands.

11 Cf. Deuteronomy 23:8-9, Amos 9:11-12, and Act 15:15-17 on the complex, special opening for reconciliation still for Edom, the seed of Jacob's twin brother Esau who, possessed of the birthright!, was rejected *afterward*, says Hebrews 12:17.

12 The most help for this last way of reading Numbers 22-24 came from: S.G. de Graaf, "In the Wilderness," *Promise and Deliverance* (St. Catharines, Ont.: Paideia Press, 1977), I, pp.327-380; W. H. Gispen, *Het Boek Numeri* [The Book of Numbers] (Kampen, the Netherlands: J. H. Kok, 1964), pp. 60-140; and J. Schelhaas, *Bileam de waarzegger-profeet* [Balaam: Soothsayer-Prophet] (Franeker, the Netherlands: T. Wever, 1935), 80 pp.

Also useful were the following: B. Holwerda, "Kaïn-Bileam-Korach" (Judas 11) in *Tot de dag aanlicht* [Till the Day Breaks] (Goes: the Netherlands: Oosterbaan & Le Cointre, 1950), pp. 274-292; Nic. H. Ridderbos, "Israël's profetie en 'profetie' buiten Israel" [Prophesy inside Israel and "Prophecy" outside of Israel], *Exegetica*, II, 1, pars. 16-18; K. Schilder, "Kerk eer dan 'vakorganisatie' " [Church before "Labour Union"], in *De Openbaring van Johannes en het sociale leven* [The Apocalypse of John and Societal Life] (Delft, the Netherlands: Naamloze Vennootschap W.D. Meinema, third printing), chapter 7.

13 There is possibly an etymological play on names here. Nicolaus, which means "people-enslaver," is practically a hellenized reproduction of Bileam, which means "people-destroyer."

14 So-called "conservatives" should not take comfort from all these remarks. "Conservatives" who read the Bible with a moralistic veil over the eyes, who want to hold the line at Victorian morality and thought patterns of outdated rationalism, who frequently only consolidate the work of "liberals" two generations later—their "orthodoxy" is no substitute for a living obedience to the Word.

But Balaam is Sadducean, not Pharisaic.

Afterword

The three or four ways of reading Scripture noted in the first edition of 1968 persist in 2003 AD a generation later. Let me comment on that phenomenon. It's hard for a leopard to change its spots, and it is apparently just as difficult for people to change their habit of reading the Bible.

The formats for reading Scripture, which I named as fundamentalistic, higher-critical humanistic, and scholastic, or better, dogmatic, may have altered their actual findings somewhat, but these diverse methodologies have remained true to form. And each format seems to foreclose on the reader's hearing certain important matters of the text that are muted by one's adopted method of Bible reading. Such blinkered reading of Scripture, of whatever stripe, is unfortunate, because everyone wants to read the Bible with personal integrity and professional care, discerning what is true and relevant.

Believing readers also want to be faithful and fully open to what God is saying through the text. A person must avoid the temptation to oversimplify the complex unity of the whole Bible. You try to catch whatever the clear, poignant point of Scripture is in a given passage, yet let the overtones sounding throughout the whole booked Word of God resonate in what you hear in a specific pericope.

I have found that it invigorates one's faith to be among followers of Christ from quite varied cultural backgrounds and sharply different societal circumstances who are trying to pray for the Lord's help in present difficulties. Pain shared in faith sharpens one's ear to hear God's comfort.

Can we also learn from what seem to us to be mistaken, wrong-headed approaches to reading the Bible? If we do not ourselves happen to be fundamentalists, higher-critical scholars, radical feminist or liberationist theologians in our precommitment to picking up the Bible, and think we can discern the veil over the others' eyes as they parse the biblical message (cf. II Corinthians

3:14-18), can that exercise teach us, Western Christians who would be obedient to the LORD's Word, to hear God speak from the Bible so we ourselves repent and humbly have our eyes opened, ears attuned, hands and feet readied anew (cf. Psalm 119:17-24) to obey the Scriptural imperative to prepare for the LORD's Rule acoming?

Higher-critical deconstruction

The source-critical reading of Numbers 22-24 continues unabated in established circles like the Anchor Bible series.[1] Tireless scholarly detective work has been expended to track down background details in the story. For example, an Aramaic writing discovered in 1967 in the Jordan valley at Deir 'Alla, which refers to the exorcist Balaam Beorson, needs to be dated and wondered about: how did such a non-Israelite figure come to be featured in the Bible? Since Moses is not mentioned in Numbers 22-24, since the Moabite point of view is taken here, and since chapters 22-24 are hardly connected to chapters 21 and 25 (25 which picks up where 21 left off), Levine and Rouillard find that this highly parodic section of three chapters really does not fit in the Pentateuch. They ask, what has the seer Balaam being mocked by a talking ass and a Moabite king using curses for weapons to do with the exodus of God's people from Egypt and their conquest of Canaan?

Levine, Rouillard and Gross all recognize now that attributing Jahwist, Elohist, and Priestly scribes to various bits of the Numbers 22-24 narrative and four poems is arbitrary and overall unconvincing, even though they rehearse and adjust the hypothesis! *El* is the proper name of Balaam's god, says Levine, and the only mention of Yahweh in 23:21 and 24:6 shows that *Yahweh*, under Moses' influence perhaps, is being "admitted to a regional pantheon" of *El* literature (4B:221). The current generation of higher-critical expositors no longer believes that J and E were schools of oral traditions that somehow were merged; now it is presumed that various **written** pre-texts were being spliced and interwoven by a series of later editors to arrive at what became canonic.

What is valuable about source-critical interpretation of the Bible is its meticulous attention to detail, and a sharp awareness that the narrative is an edited text rather than something that dropped cold out of heaven. However, because the historical-critical method brackets out the unifying story of the whole Bible and seems to ignore the actual God-speaking character of the Scriptures, this method stares the narrative down into mostly details, as if one were reading the text through a microscope. Rather than appreciate the world-historical scope of the covenantal Lord God's deeds for God's people among the nations and in confrontation with the subtle machinations of demonic forces (cf. above p. 44), the higher-critical reading of Numbers 22-24 misses the dynamic true story of God's overruling a conflicted seer with animal and Angel to save Israel from real disaster so close to the Promised Land, and leaves us with an editors' cut-and-paste puzzle of incongruous details.

In my judgment it is a mistake to treat nuanced features of narrative as if they be fragments from heterogeneous sources, and then deconstruct a masterfully told tale into a mix of certified facts and literary flourishes of disparate pre-texts. I admire the impeccable scholarship of Anchor Bible research but find the results sometimes beside the point.[2] Higher-critical reading of Scripture can have the dispassionate seriousness of a good dentist drilling in teeth to fix cavities; we need dependable dentistry in order to have a good bite and to develop normative mouth hygiene. Such assiduous professional attention uncovers and certifies important historical facts and literary nuances for reading aright. But to treat the biblical text first of all as an archaeological dig in which you must discover, date and identify each fascinating piece of rubble but neglect to get at the artefact in its integrality is a lamentable failing of such scholarship. A person can learn a lot in following this method, but unless you use it propadeutically as supplement, you may miss the pearl of great price: hearing God speak.

Dogmatic filtering: The liberationist angle

The scholastic, schooled reading of Scripture concerned to press the Bible for its doctrines is also carried on today. Roman Catholic, Lutheran, Reformed theologians and other christian faith-thought traditions often have their favorite Bible passages up front and in reserve, and seem able to distill from most books of the Bible the main planks of their respective systematic theologies.[3]

Focussing Bible reading on dogmatic tenets has spawned new orthodoxies too, partly because the old christian orthodox readings seem somewhat rationalistically dated today, not hip to our skeptical, do-it cultural temper, which is tuned to partisan minority voices. A quite self-consciously dogmatic way of reading the Bible nowadays is a feminist reading; or, cast in a larger community of interpretation, there is what might be called an approach intent upon proving the subversive dialectic of the holy scriptures: God is on the side of the oppressed.

I have not been able to find a prototypical feminist interpretation of Numbers 22-24, probably because those chapters lack the thematic material that could prompt specific prophylactic points against disparaging women.[4] The *Women's Bible Commentary* does observe that in Numbers 25 it is Moabite and Midianite **women** who are considered the seductive villains who lead Israel astray, and that earlier (in chapter 12) Miriam was unfairly punished next to Aaron for challenging Moses' leadership because he had married a black Cushite woman.[5] Such remarks, though, illustrate what may be the too narrow a focus of feminism for gathering in the societal life-changing power of God's booked Word—which is precisely what believing feminists rightly want to do—to reform the oppression and abuse of women and children throughout the world.

Although it may be fanciful to give a Marxian reading of Numbers 22-24, it is worthwhile to take seriously the way the many oppressed groups of people like women and two-thirds world persecuted Christians read Scripture, those who have hardly had a voice to be heard until of late (cf. illustratiom A).

(A) Jennifer Hillenga, Seen but not heard (1997)
Collection of Inès and Calvin Naudin ten Cate-Seerveld

The artist Jennifer Hillenga (b. 1976) portrays how so many women in the church have felt and do feel, as if they have no voice on matters that count. Many men continue to treat women like children who should be seen but not heard when it comes to ordering worship and proclaiming God's Word. Until women are also seen "in the Lord" (I Corinthians 11:11-12) to have mouths which speak—God's Word has always encouraged them to tell the deeds of the Lord—their eyes should haunt ecclesiastical powers with this unreal silence in Christ's body.

Their heterodox orthodoxies can make a strong corrective contribution to our standard, bland, Western churchly reading of the Bible. Yet it is fascinating to see how recent revolutionary readings of the Bible quickly assume a rather formulaic mould and the posture of certainty as to the biblical message, which many felt characterized the inflexible, unctuous doctrinal stance of earlier conservative orthodoxy.

A subversive reading of Numbers 22-24 would certainly highlight the weakness of the tired tribes of Israelite men, women, children, and cattle exposed on the plains of Moab (22:1). God is always on the side of the poor; so God put fear into the hearts of Moab royalty. True to form, the Mid-Eastern Moabite empire hires a famed, pricey diviner as sorcerer to put a whammy on this "special" spiritual folk (22:2-6). So the classic opposition between a covenanted community seeking liberation under Moses from enslavement in Egypt and another clique of political powerbrokers takes place.

This struggle presages the perennial war which happened also within Israel later on: the imperial Solomonic reign claiming God's Messianic approval for the house of David whose kings were continually opposed by prophets such as Nathan, Elijah, Amos, Isaiah and Jeremiah, who spoke the upsetting Word of the Lord against the dynastic status quo. Jesus too attacked the Sadducee and Pharisee temple establishment ideology, and left it to the apostle Paul to carry on as "troubler of Israel" (I Kings 18:17-19) against encrusted Rabbinic Judaism. Needed today are not highly paid consultants like Balaam at ecumenical conferences, but prophetic leaders from the people who will challenge the ecclesial, bureaucratic guild of theologians with the good news of empowerment to the poor![6]

Attractive about this updated militant, dogmatic way of reading Scripture is its taking up cudgels for the dispossessed and wretched of the earth, those who have been neglected or trampled underfoot by the minions of corporate power in state, church, or business. The Bible does say unequivocably that injustice towards others is sin, and merciless exploitation of the weak must be ended on pain of severe judgment against the unjust. **All** of us who are members of the societal system run by a Darwinian survival-of-the-fittest principality are guilty before God on this score, especially if we tacitly accept our privileges.

But the flaw to the subversive focus in reading the Bible is its localization of evil in the institutionalization of power. Then the powerless are taken at face value as anonymous saints, the poor cannot themselves be greedy, and outcasts will never have a vindictive heart. Such a utopian thesis is wrong, and blunts our hearing God speak the full biblical counsel. Whenever Scripture is read to say, "We disenfranchised people have a God-given right to subvert those who wield unholy power in society," Scripture is pawned to a dialectical hermeneutic of **us** against **them**, which skews the gospel in a lop-sided manner, off-center, like squinting with one eye. Then **we** liberators have God's point of view for what **others**, the oppressors, must do. **We** are left off the hook.

But the Bible's call to do justice is never congratulatory, and it eschews self-righteous rhetoric. God's Word pins us down to a response of doing good in return for evil (Romans 12:9-21), of faithfully bringing God's will to fruition indiscriminately (Matthew 25:31-46), of suffering patiently for the long haul while expecting God to vindicate the meek (Matthew 5:1-20). That is, God is not on the side of the poor anymore than God is on the side of good bourgeois people. God in Jesus Christ is on the side of sinful human creatures who become repentant followers of the Christ, no matter what their well-being or sad status in society be.

The trace of biblical truth in the liberationist dogmatic filtering of Scripture is the echo of Hannah's prayer (I Samuel 2:1-10) and Mary's exultation (Luke 1:46-55) about the LORD God's looking out for those who have great need but no voice in the circles of might and vanity. Those who hear God speak in Hannah and Mary's prayers in Scripture cannot rest until justice **and peace** permeate the whole land (Amos 5:24), since God is not a respecter of persons (Acts 10:34-35): rough shepherds and the cultured wise are welcome in God's Rule; outcast lepers **and** the manipulative rich like Zaccheus are able to repent in deed and receive grace. The oppressed do not have a corner on the gospel.

The misstep taken by liberationist readers is to disconnect poverty and riches, power and powerlessness in the Bible from being coloured by the humbled or proud stance humans cut before God. The abbreviated version of Matthew 5 ("Blessed are the poor in spirit," 5:3) and Matthew 23 found in Luke 6 ("Blessed are you poor," 6:20b) is not substantively different in thrust: God blesses men, women and children who hunger for the LORD's right-doing, and God curses those who heartlessly take care of themselves at the expense of their neighbor (cf. Isaiah 57:15, Luke 16:14-15). The crux for Scripture is never **simply** phenomenal; what the Bible does show is that the "rich" Laodiceans are more than metaphorically "poor" (Revelation 3:14-22), and those followers of Christ whom secular society considers "poverty-stricken" may be truly "rich" adopted children of God (Proverbs 10:22, I Corinthians 4:7-8, II Corinthians 6:8b-10, 8:9).

Just as one cannot know God unless you are obeying God, so a person cannot read Scripture aright on "freeing the oppressed" without confessing **in deed** that we who are clothed and housed and have daily food are "the rich" whom the Bible anathematizes unless we are caught in the act of giving away our clothes to the naked, exercising hospitality to the hungry, and going the extra mile in reading Scripture till God's voice convicts us of our own complicity in the regime of wanting MORE, so we are driven in repentant hope to quiet systemic, communal deeds of mercy.

The simple gospel: Jesus saves

A fundamentalistic reading of the Bible continues apace since many Christians still want an uncomplicated faith in God. The meaning resides straightforwardly in the biblical text and simply needs to be distilled: God created the world; humans fell into sin; the Son of God, Jesus Christ, was born of the virgin Mary, suffered, died under Pontius Pilate, was resurrected from the dead, ascended to God's right hand, sent the Holy Spirit to earth as Comforter until we believers go to heaven or Jesus comes back in glory. What more does one need to know?

The fundamentals about sin and salvation are crucial to a biblically christian cast to one's life and consciousness. If one stays only with the fundamentals, however, the richness of the christian faith is not discovered, biblical tenets tend to shrivel into dicta, the Older Testament is neglected as superceded history, and believers can remain immature, with the best of intentions. Bible reading then becomes like a worship service in which only Bible **choruses** are sung, but never whole psalms. You still paint the house, but there is so much thinner in the paint that the colour becomes watery.

A good example of keeping Bible reading simple is *The Living Bible* translation (1971), touted as "Not Just Another Version," but one which "has become a model for translations throughout the world," a phenomenal commercial success in the USA throughout the 1970s.[7] Its method of translation was to paraphrase the meaning found in the original Hebraic and Greek languages: "to say it simply and with flavor, expanding where necessary for a clear understanding by the modern reader [in English]." Kenneth Taylor's guiding principle was "to simplify the deep and often complex thoughts of the Word of God," to make the Bible "easier to understand and follow." The Living Bible simplifies the Bible especially to reach "individuals outside of the churches who would never, otherwise, read a Bible," persons in prisons, for example, or those whom Wycliffe Bible Translators want to reach around the world.

Good about making certain the basic thrust of the Bible is kept in view—God was in Christ reconciling the world back to God self (II Corinthians 5:19)—is that a Bible reader is not encouraged to get lost in details or to run stuck on minor points. A danger, however, in simplifying the biblical message is to get the crux of the gospel **oversimplified**. "Jesus saves … me and you" is not wrong, but such an individualistic reduction of the biblical message from its cosmic scope is not right either: "God so loved the **whole world** of creation, including us special human creatures, God sent the Son … so that **the world** and everything in it which belongs to the Lord (Psalm 24:1-2) and is suffering from our sin (Romans 8:9-25) might be saved" (John 3:16-17).

The method of evangelistic simplification, intent upon reaching "seekers" looking for help or an escape from our worldly miseries, in language they will understand, can succumb to the temptation to turn the Bible into a tract. For example, *The Living Bible*'s rendition of Romans 1:16-17 simplifies God's Word to a fundamentalistic cliché, as if "salvation" and "righteousness" is "getting to heaven"!

> *For I am not ashamed of this Good News about Christ. It is God's powerful method of bringing all who believe it to heaven. . . . This Good News tells us that God makes us ready for heaven—makes us right in God's sight—when we put our faith and trust in Christ to save us. . . .*

Such a "popular translation" betrays the thrust of Scripture to newcomers and will let them **mis**understand God's word for "being saved" and "God's right-doing" (*dikaiosuné*). The truthful call to live a difficult, true-dealing life out of Christ's saving a person that is heard in "The just shall live by faith" (King James, 1:17b)—those who are justified sheerly by Christ and do justice on the earth live out of faith—is obscured by the paraphrase "God makes us ready for heaven. . . . The man who finds life will find it through trusting God" (Living Bible, 1:17)—as if one could "find life" and can close one's eyes to the world needing our care.

It is a mistake to read the Bible too fast, as if it were today's newspaper followed by other dispatches tomorrow, since the Bible as book is not an easy read. The Bible is **profoundly** simple, perspicuous but deserving and needing study, because the Bible is God-speaking **literature** and not a body of simple sentences. Reading the Bible for many is like reading a foreign language. We should not custom fit the radical, earth-shaking textual meaning of the Bible to a current-day reader's expectations and naive response which are unfamiliar with the biblical world, as if "modern" man's earthbound reach should be determinative. It would be better, I think, to let the upsetting strangeness of the

(B)

Pablo Picasso, Crucifixion (1930)

Collection of the artist

The Spanish artist Pablo Picasso (1881-1973) is a master at deconstructing figures into fragments, which details are then conceptually scattered to fascinate the viewer. The small white Christ in this crucifixion painting is practically lost to sight behind the open-jawed white apostle John crying while reclining on Jesus' breast amid the melee of dead thieves on the ground, soldiers throwing dice for the cloak, the blood-stained ladder, smirking onlooker and more. The main events of Golgotha are all there but dispersed and added to–a miniature picador is thrown in for good measure–a collage of sources not focussed by the one historical truth of Christ's finishing the task for which God became incarnate (John 19:28-30). A person who reads the painting is left with a universe of notes that spell "Awful Dislocation in general."

Bible's message be present in the translation and be teased out slowly bit by bit for the inquisitive person through a Spirit-informed **oral guide** who knows what the Lord is saying in the biblical thesaurus (cf. evangelist Phillip with the Ethiopian eunuch, Acts 8:26-40). The Bible has meat to it, and God asks all readers who start by drinking the basic milk of the gospel (formulated in the Apostle's creed) to mature, lest one shortchange what God has given us to grow on (Hebrews 5:11-6:2).

Ongoing Reformational christian faith orientation

The biblically Reformational reading of Scripture I spoke up for thirty years ago (cf. above pp. 39-40) still commends itself to me as honest to God, supple and rich as a method which, given one reads the Bible on one's knees, so to speak, provides a hermeneutic avenue that bears good communal fruit: it helps us read the Bible to hear God speak. And the Lord God is not a harp with just one string, but a whole orchestra of sound that voices *chesed, 'emet, chokmah, mishphat, aphesis, agapé, eulogia,* and *shalom.*

I continue to appreciate the painstaking rigor of **higher-critical scholarship**, which leaves no stone unturned to ferret out historical referents and literary nuances. I just lament the initial Neopositivist and Idealist temper of detachment that informed its exposition, always holding God at arm's length, as it were, lest one lose "scientific objectivity" and be convicted by the message. Current higher-critical practitioners have hardened into the error, it seems to me, of dismissing the crucial contextually informing true story of God's deeds which the Bible tells, and of rejecting the childlikeness proper for Bible reading. Therefore the current generation of expert higher-critical scholars seem to slip into an intelligent skepsis that chases minutiae endlessly (cf. illustration B) rather than struggle to discern knowledge outfitted with understanding on how to live biblically in our troubled days.

(C) Francisco de Zurbaran, St. Veronica's Veil (1600s)
National Museum of Sweden

Catholic legend has it that the face of Jesus was miraculously imprinted on a cloth. The Spanish church artist Francisco de Zurbaran (1598-1664) depicts this ghostly appearance most exactly: sorrowful eyes, furrowed brow under a hint of thorns, lips parted in exhaustion, but in a handsome face unmarred by historical specificity. Since God's glory is to be found in Jesus' face (II Corinthians 4:6), its essential features must reveal a perfect serenity. Zurburan tucks the venerated face neatly into cloth material folded in a beautiful manner just a touch too elegantly symmetrical to be true.

What is worthy in the old style **dogmatically pressured reading** is the constancy of the doctrines elicited from the biblical texts. A range of determinate meanings is not in question, and after studying passages of the Bible a faithful reader has a bird in the hand rather than different possible birds still disseminated in the bush. Amid the erosion of certainties in our secularized culture, reaffirmation of traditional dogmas can be satisfying. Disconcerting, however, is the eisegetical maneuver which legitimates the time-honoured tenets of particular ecclesial communions (cf. illustration C), tenets which have led to church splitting, suppression of reformers, and unholy wars that discredit the very God of the Scriptures one is fighting for.

The current liberationist tilt to a dogmatic reading of the Bible moves an educated person to hear notes of God's voice formerly lost in the Constantinian edition of Western establishmentarian Christianity, which has been willing and able for centuries to dispense Bibles and exploitive colonial Rule together. But the trouble with **the liberationist prejudice** is that its Bible begins with Exodus instead of Genesis, the charismatic prophet is cast as anti-royal-establishment, Jesus is made over into a revolutionary martyr (cf. illustration D), and the dogma of perpetual subversive activity displaces the good news of the Lord God's mysterious, ironic election of the weak outcasts of the world to work out God's will (cf. Matthew 5:1-20, I Corinthians 1:18-2:5, Philippians 1:27-2:16).

The **simple Bible readers** rightly listen for God to speak because they want to obey the LORD and make the pure gospel available to disbelievers. But often such readers seem to read the Bible in a time warp, a century out of date (cf. illustration E), and hear God speak with a comfortable middle-class accent. Fundamentalist readers are usually uncritical of their presuppositions, and unknowingly subscribe to the practicalist heresy that if you know what's good, you will do it—with Jesus' help, of course. Such well-meaning, pious reading gives me a heartache because it tends to package "the christian faith made easy, in three or four steps," and then cannot prepare converts to face the

(D)

Jose Clemente Orozco, Christ destroys his cross (1943)

Museo de Arte Carrillo Gil, Mexico

In the revolutionary vision of the Mexican Jose Clemente Orozco (1883-1947) the heroic Christ takes an ax to the cross of the classical Roman empire. Holy books also go up in fire if they promise a blood-stained instrument of torture to be the way to save Humanity. After all, did not Christ himself say to the corrupt, money-changing establishment, "Destroy this temple[which has] become a marketplace!" (John 2:13-22) At least that is the way the false witnesses understood it (Matthew 26:59-62).

horrendous complications of historical sin and the unintended consequences of good intentional action; so people are encouraged to hear "Jesus saves!" as the simple offer of "Rescue **from** this world," which does belong to God.

Let me draw out a little the implications of the four components to the biblical Reformational reading of holy scripture, where Scripture is taken to be God-speaking literature given us historically for our learning by faith the one true story of the Lord's Rule acoming and the contours of our obedient response.

(1) **The whole Bible is God's telling us humans the true story of the Lord's great deeds** beginning with creation, followed by the amazing historical selection of the Hebrew people who are given the covenantal promise that God will send the Messiah in David's seed to redeem the whole world. In due time God sent God's Son to be born of Mary, to suffer, die, be resurrected, and to ascend triumphantly to heaven from where God's Holy Spirit came to sustain the faithful until Jesus Christ returns to finish up eradicating sin and evil, and to put all creatures completely under the Lord's compassionate Rule (Psalm 110, Hebrews 10:11-25).

This single biblical story of the Lord God's promise and fulfillment of God's will in history is accepted through the Holy Spirit's testimony in the hearts of believers to be utterly trustworthy, an authoritative telling of what happened and is taking place. Both the Older and the Newer Testaments reinforce each other as a unity, and together both testaments serve as the constitutional canon for the church to bring this singular account of Jesus Christ's scandalous centrality clearly to the fore: the eternal God is covenantal by nature and reiterated God's faithfulness in word and deed throughout history—for Eve and Adam (Genesis 3:4-21), Noah (Genesis 9:8-17), Abraham and Sarah (Genesis 15), Moses (Exodus 19-20,24,34), David (II Samuel 7), and on to whoever become followers of the Christ and receive the Holy Spirit (Joel 2:28-32, Jeremiah 31:31-34, John 16:12-15). The riveting story line of the Lord's *magnalia Dei* through all the twists and turns of the turmoil surrounding God's chosen people is maintained.

**(E) William Holmar Hunt, The Light of the World (1853)
Keble College, Oxford, England**

The lighted lantern held by this svelte figure wearing a gold-brocaded cape as he knocks at the oaken door overgrown with weeds is British William Holmar Hunt's (1825-1919) way to ask the simple question: "Do you hear Jesus knocking today at the door of your heart?" (Luke 12:36, Revelation 3:20). The crown of thorns haloed by a harvest moon, however, seems like an overly romantic way to gentle Christ's sacrifice into a palatable evangelistic morsel.

It is important to accentuate that the Older Testament is integral to the intelligibility of this singular story from beginning to end. The earlier Older Testament has its own specific gravity as the exacting Jewish Publication Society's *Torah* commentary on *Numbers* by Jacob Milgrom (New York, 5750/1990) makes evident. Milgrom's minute examination of the received "Section of Balaam" shows by cross-references that the four poetic oracles are thoroughly embedded in the prose narrative. Milgrom exposits how the skillful composition of the piece as a whole, including the interpolated folktale of the talking ass which mocks the seer's renowned divinatory power, provides the ironic twist that instead of Moab's cursing Israel as Balak planned (Numbers 22:4-6), Moab ends up itself being cursed (Numbers 24:17). Because the presence of the LORD God is paramount in the Hexateuch tale of Israel's wilderness wandering between exodus from Egypt and entry into Canaan, Milgrom highlights the revelation that there is no divination of omens in Israel (Numbers 23:23) because God speaks directly to God's people whenever the LORD pleases, even through a Spirit-filled prophet who is not kosher (Numbers 24:2-4,15-16)!

Because Milgrom does not couch his commentary on Numbers in the one story of the **whole** Bible but only in terms of the Hebrew Scriptures, he hears only the overtones of God's journey with Israel; for example, how Balak like the Egyptian pharaoh tried three times to obstruct God's plan for Israel and thus brought devastation upon his nation too, while Israel at Baal-peor (Numbers 25) had its apostasy punished in sequel to the golden calf idolatry at Mount Sinai. But one needs to realize Numbers 21-25 is a chapter in the continuous story of God's dealings with humanity under the horizon of Jesus Christ's coming to catch the sense of momentous crisis happening here in the plains of Moab (cf. above pp. 43-44): God's cantankerous people are losing their innocence as an apprentice peoplehood and are being faced with the challenge to make governing decisions wholeheartedly for the Lord in the circle of nations, or suffer God's rejection (cf. above pp. 45-49). The Reformational christian reader notices the pattern of how this early Numbers 21-25 episode and the later chapter in the story Paul tells in Romans 9-11 reinforce one another: the LORD is a faithful jealous provider for the fitful company of believers who are judged and saved only by grace, namely, gratuitous merciful love, which came to be refocussed in the action of Jesus Christ.[8]

It should be said that what story one takes as lectional apriori for Bible reading, whether Jewish or Christian or secularist, is unarguable and predogmatic. A reader simply assumes a certain story line, usually embodied in a particular, traditioned faith community whose *regula fidei* gives the contours. The Reformation faith-thought tradition, which notes that Christ spent his last forty days on earth trying to proclaim the compassionate Rule of God (Acts 1:3) is the christian *Gestalt* in which I am grateful to belong as a Bible-reading adopted child of God.

(2) That the Bible is booked in Hebrew, Aramaic, and Greek languages, with writings BC from the distant time of Moses (Deuteronomy 31:24-29) to writings a couple of generations after Christ's death AD (Hebrews 2:1-4, 13:22-24) is also a given. Exactly when a certain portion of Scripture was written down or reached edited form is relatively important and often disputed, but any uncertainty of dated location for this or that writing does not compromise the historiographic veracity of the text.

For example, the synoptic gospels reached written form post-resurrection and after Pentecost, but their "news" of Jesus' earthly deeds is reported in the historical present tense because there were eyewitnesses. The apostle Paul's various letters were occasioned by real troubles and disputes in quite different churches; they were straightforward rhetorical missives meant to bring healing and godly order into the lives of Jews and gentiles intent upon following the crucified and risen Messiah. Who knows who scripted Genesis 1-11, Deuteronomy 34, II Samuel 23-24, and the book to the Hebrews? Our limited knowledge about the dated amanuensis is not determinative for our being able to trust what is written because the Bible is **God speaking** and not just the witness of Spirit-empowered humans. The Bible is **God making**

known in a fascinating number of prophetic ways (Hebrews 1:l) that God is the covenantal Lord God Yahweh become incarnate in Jesus Christ to set creation right again (II Corinthians 5:17-19).

The colourful human writers God used to tell this historical truth all followed Greek medical doctor Luke's method of **drawing up a narrative account of what has been fulfilled among them, to write it down exactly, so that we readers might know precisely with reliability the things we have been told** (Luke 1:1-4). The biblical scribes, breathed upon by God's Spirit (II Timothy 3:16-17), fashioned word portraits of *ephapax* (once-only) events that happened and cast the Word of God in skillful literary formulations which are not a whit less true, with ostensive referents, than the xerox documentary photographs or tape recordings a Positivist would demand. But Moses, Nathan, David, Isaiah, the apostles, and others were not European Positivists of the 1800s AD. The history-telling of holy scripture is never just archival data because **the script is God-speaking** about certain actualities (indicative) and what God's deeds and the human responses inscribed mean **for us readers today on how to respond to the LORD** (imperative).

Because the history kept by the Bible is simultaneously revelation by God, the "plain meaning" of the text (*sensus literalis*) is quite matter-of-factly informative to the faith-community that recognizes its Lord's voice. Even to those who are still strangers to God's confidences, the Bible is clearly telling things as they are in an idiom that a person can grasp once you are given the key to the vernacular of the book (which the Pharisees! had thrown away, cf. Luke 11:52). Philo and Origen's allegorical expository meaning found *above* the text and higher-critical fascination with (speculative, reconstructed) meaning *below* the text distracted readers from the very text in front of them and undermined its apparent meaning. The Reformation of Luther and Calvin declared "the plain meaning" of the text to be the veritable correct scriptural meaning (*verus scripturae sensus*) God wanted us to hear. "The plain meaning" refers to what is idiomatic in a given culture, in which language keeps its colour and overtones and does not promote **literalistic** reading, where words are stared down at as if they were anagrammatic counters.[9]

So, of course, live angels and real devils carry out their destructive deeds (II Kings 19:35-37, Matthew 8:28-34) in time on earth; snakes and asses can be mouthpieces for communicating God's messages (Genesis 3:1-7, Numbers 22:21-35); miracles and the conversion of persecutors of God's people into missionary saints (John 2:1-11, Acts 9:1-22) are historical facts without becoming statistics. If the resurrection of the dead Jesus Christ is an historical happening, as it indeed is (Luke 24, John 20-21), why can the Creator God of the universe not do other surprising things, which God's children are grateful to know took place once upon a time?

(3) The historical embeddedness of the biblical writings does not preclude their literary finish. That the Bible is God-speaking literature is crucial to the reader's being able to hear God speak through the scripted word. Many people today are literate, but when it comes to the Bible they are "illiterary": they mistakenly think you tamper with the truth of Scripture if you do not read the Bible like a telephone book which lists a collection of verses for certified doctrines, prescriptions for sanctification, or phone-a-prayer type quotations. But **God has had the Bible booked as literature, which has an imaginative quality defining its overall character.**

Even sections like Leviticus or the recitation of survivors from exile in Nehemiah 7 and genealogies in Genesis 5 and Matthew 1 are not just row upon row of legal statutes and (in)accurate records of births and deaths: such texts are imbricated in the single story told from Genesis 1 to Revelation 21. The point of those texts is the providing faithfulness of the LORD God to the third and the fourth and the thousandth generation of sinful, outcast saints God prefers to involve in the Lord's upside-down, historic Rule of sheer grace (cf. Acts 14:5-6, I Corinthians 1:18-2:5).

Literature makes imaginative sense while it refers to realities both visible and invisible that never cross the radar screen of a scientific technician or startle a Positivist's eyeball. Numbers

22-24, for example, tells the story of what actually happened, including the overlapping anger of God toward Balaam (22:22), Balaam's anger toward the ass (22:27), and Balak's anger toward Balaam (24:10), and how Balaam still connived to devastate God's people (25:1-9, 31:1-20), although the final blessing of the LORD God overruled the punishment (24:17, cf. Deuteronomy 23:5, Nehemiah 13:2). The allusive quality to a literary text can nuance Balaam's respectable avarice, Israel's unsuspecting vulnerability, the fastidious correctness of the sacrifices performed to twist God's arm; it can portray precisely the flexible, enigmatic way the eternal LORD God gives us humans the room to obey God or hurt ourselves.

A literary account of origins and endings can be wonderfully and properly elusive, as the biblical Genesis and book of Revelation are. It is a faulty philosophical aesthetics which would destroy that mystery and rationalistically demand that the Bible be either factual or fictional, either mythical or reportorial. Genesis should not be pressed to answer questions it doesn't entertain. And *tertia datur.* Revelation is not a timetable of millennium disasters or mythical fantasy: it is literature framing knowledge of comfort for historically beleaguered saints provided with the suggestion-rich lilt of a parent telling a child the truth of something which will become more clear later on.

It is helpful for learning to read the Bible to take a cue from the offhand remark the resurrected Jesus made to the Cleopas couple on their walk to Emmaeus and later on to Christ's disciples: **the scriptures confess him in the law of Moses, the prophets and the psalms** (Luke 24:27,44). That is, it was normal already in Jesus' day to distinguish within the Older canon the historiographic writings of "Moses" whom the LORD God used to table God's law, the prophets from Samuel through Malachi, and the "writings" (*ketubim*) as the Psalms, the festival rolls (Song of Songs, Ruth, Lamentations, Ecclesiastes and Esther) and the fantastic visionary chapters of Daniel were called. One could delineate the Newer Testament canonic texts in a similar way: the Gospels and Acts of the apostles' history-telling, the prophetic letters of Paul, Peter, James, John and Jude for reflection on disputable matters, and poetic writings like Hebrews and the visionary Revelation.

All these various sorts of texts are God-speaking literature, but to hear **God** speak through the formulation one must recognize that David's lament for the dead Saul and Jonathan (II Samuel 1:17-27) is different in temper from Nehemiah's diary on reconstructing Jerusalem's wall. One needs to study the progression of Paul's sustained argument to the Jews and Gentiles in Rome from Romans chapters 1 to 8 (around 3:21-31), then the extraordinary reassessment of history in chapters 9 to 11, followed by the rhetorically phrased injunctions of chapters 12 to 15, in order to hear **God's** pleading with believers then and now not to follow their noses with work-righteousness, but to learn the graceful freedom of living God-dependently thankful. A person is apt to miss **God's** voice if you don't realize The Song of Songs is a unified chorus of different voices, that the book of Ecclesiastes has a sevenfold refrain which is the clue to unlock its flavor of rejoicing in God's gifts under terrible pressure; a reader needs to see that the collection of wise Proverbs are in paragraphs rather than atomic one-liners, if you want to catch **God's** message in this epigrammatic literature.[10]

It is precisely this variegated literary character of God's Word booked that higher-critical literary analysis uses to fragment and violate the integrity of the canon, when it is exactly this rich variety of witnessing narrative, authoritative instruction, "Thus-says-the-LORD" prophecy, experiential praise, gritty laments, and the reflectional struggles of God's children that constitute the canon and bespeak the incredible, compassionate, myriad wisdom of the Lord, continually surprising the attentive readers waiting to hear God speak.

(4) The linchpin for reading the Bible in this Reformational christian way is indeed to remember that **this God-speaking literature** given us historically with the overarching story of the Christ's Rule acoming **as book is meant to be heard. The Bible is a script to become oral. The writing is by nature**

kerygmatic, a live telling, a proclaiming which asks those within hearing for a decisive response now. The Bible is the inscripturation of God speaking.

So, when the Bible is read rightly, God speaks, to readers in the vocative case. When God speaks, every creature is bound to become still and listen to God's voice (cf. Psalm 29). The God-speaking Bible is unique in this respect and is not simply an instantiation of a broad category of confessional scriptures held by certain people to be "sacred," like the *Qur'an, Bhagavad-Gita*, or the *Book of Mormon* for millions of Mormon believers. That's the scandal of the Bible and its compelling power. Just as only Jesus Christ was God-man human, so only the Bible is God-speaking writing.

As Holy Spirit breathed scripture (II Peter 1:20-21), in its witness throughout the ages to the saving work of Jesus Christ, the Bible says it is God's gift to us who read so that we may receive "a disciplined training in right-doing" (II Timothy 3:16-17), that is, have our very consciousness (*nous*) set in the LORD's way of doing things (cf. Ephesians 6:4). Or, as the Older Testament puts it, the textual deposit is here so we humans may learn the discipline (*musar*) of insightful action, namely, be seasoned with wisdom to act with integrity, justly, without guile (Proverbs 1:2-6), that is, "to become a mediating loving person in the order of Melchizedek" (Psalm 110:4, Hebrews 7:1-8:2, I Peter 2:9-10)—Christ-like! (cf. illustration F). **The Scriptures give us**, to use John Calvin's metaphor (*Institutio Christianae religionis*, I,6,1), the "**eye-glasses**" **to read God's creational revelation aright**. Bible-reading becomes like having God-speaking at your side as you scrutinize creatural order to discern God's will for acting with obedience in any field of endeavor, shaping societal institutions, reforming historical mistakes, exploring uncharted waters.

So the God-speaking biblical script gives readers direction, vision, a head start in leading a daily life in God's world with meaning that lasts. The Bible is not meant to be read just "theologically," so one gets his or her creeds and doctrines straight, or

((F)

Emil Nolde, Christ among the Children (1910)

Museum of Modern Art, New York, U.S.A.

German artist Emil Nolde (1867-1956) shows the Christ enveloped by a swarm of colour-exuberant children alive with response to Jesus' attention. Despite the disapproving, stolid looks of the male disciples, the artwork is a joyous painting. Christ's blue-green back bent toward the sea of red, orange and yellow dark-haired children goes deep into the rich joy of the Good News (Mark 10:13-16). Work-righteous kill-joys do not understand that shalom is a free gift of God's grace.

to download a program for evangelistic outreach, worthy as such activity be. An introverted "theological" restriction to the existential kerygmatic directional character of the Bible would curtail its performative reach and stunt its power to redirect societal life, to posit alternatives to political dead ends, to redeem commercialistic idolatry with stewardly principles geared to generosity. When the range of God-speaking is fully heard and understood to be the focussing Word for doing creatural tasks, then the LORD's Word permeates and changes all kinds of things and turns crooked policies as well as policy makers around into stalwart leaders and deeds of shalom at large.

Once one knows the Bible is God-speaking literature, Paul's cautionary note about "not going beyond what is written" (I Corinthians 4:6) provides the insight on how we readers are to remain subject to the writing rather than presume as Spirit-filled believers we stand over the text as its master-interpreters (cf. illustration G). The right attitude for reading the Bible is to take seriously that **we are spoken to**, we Bible readers are **listeners**, the subjective **objects of God's** face-to-face, as it were, **talking to**. The live wire nature of the Bible asks us readers to be open to what the text, as God's mouthpiece, says, and when the Scriptures say something which goes against our grain, against our received ideas and considered expectations, then we are to take it in even more carefully, because God is probably trying to pry open our heart even if we are hard of hearing.

A good way to get the God-speaking literature oral is to read it aloud. And once you have a good sense of what the LORD is saying, read it aloud with understanding—reading is the primal (aesthetic) interpretation (*hermeneuein*) of written texts—in public, for people, because then the Bible's convicting power to reach all tribes and nations and generations in normal and abnormal circumstances becomes evident. When a faithful human re-speaks the biblical writing, others will join the speaking, sing along, dance a joyful response, shout "Thanks be to God!" "LORD, be merciful to me," or else put one's hands over one's ears.[11]

CREDULITY, SUPERSTITION, and FANATICISM.
A MEDLEY.
Believe not every Spirit but try the Spirits whether they are of God: because many false Prophets are gone out into the World.
1 John. Ch.4 V.1.
Design'd and Engrav'd by Wm. Hogarth. Publish'd as the Act directs March ye 15th 1762.

(G) William Hogarth, Credulity, Superstition, Fanaticism, A Medley Collection of Inès and Calvin Naudin ten Cate-Seerveld (1762)

This engraving by British William Hogarth (1697-1764) pokes fun at revivalist preachers whose enthusiasm and audio-visual aids run away with them as they whip up a crowd to extraordinary emotional heights and strange ecstasies. But Hogarth's text is serious (I John 4:1), and reminds every Bible reader to test the spirit of those who act "the prophetic voice" with God's scriptures, calling attention to themselves rather than to the Word of the LORD which does not need human histrionics to be heard.

* * *

There is no easy trick to learn how to read the Bible to hear God speak. If one does not believe holy scripture is the veritable source for hearing the Lord God talk to us, then one is cut off from the miracle of the Bible even before one starts. The most basic condition for Bible reading to be operative is the (believing) desire to listen to what the text proclaims. Then it helps to have a sound, methodical way to go about our reading the book together as one matures in the faith. It is also crucial to realize that one is not supposed to stare just at the Bible: we must let the God-speaking biblical writings sound in our ears and heart as we examine the glossolalia speech of God's world. Otherwise you hear God speak in a vacuum chamber.[12]

Given the four components of the Reformational christian perspective that I have articulated, it becomes clear why the other three ways of Bible reading I have delineated seem to me to have short-comings. The higher-critical approach virtually omits a single, guiding storyline, focusses all its attention on literary, historical items, appears uninterested in the kerygmatic dimension of the Bible, and is fairly content with an ivory tower existence. The dogmatically focussed readers go almost single-mindedly for the theological/manifesto dogmas dear to their hearts, embrace them with prophetic authority—for example, God is a trinity, or, the oppressed are God's elect—and find that special doctrine to be the basic skeleton of the storyline dictated by the raging war in the world between orthodoxy and the heretics, between the haves and the have-nots. The simple Bible readers jump from a "Jesus saves!" storyline to the authoritative preaching step and avoid most historical, literary analysis, and seem inhibited from having Scriptural light shine upon all the reality waiting for our cultivation but instead listen for instructions on how to prepare for going to heaven.

While I am ready to say, in the manner of Paul, that whatever hermeneutical method one is using, if it somehow leads to the proclamation of Jesus Christ's saving Rule acoming in God's world, I can be glad about that (cf. Philippians 1:15-18). But the lectional astigmatism I find marring these other methods—despite what they make me thankfully aware of—is disturbing because the biblical "eye-glasses" they give people for viewing reality are sorely out of focus; they do not help people hear and see and do the full counsel of God (cf. Acts 20:17-35) with a thankful heart.

Fruitful about the Reformational christian prospectus for Bible reading is its certainty about the basic storyline that Jesus Christ died for our sin, to redeem God's world, confirmed by an incredible concordance of resonances throughout the Older and Newer Testament scriptures. In that certainty, the reader is wide open to being surprised by revelation of God's recorded actions, which are not logical, not even reasonable, but often scandalous. For example, as the Bible tells it, God let the devil loose in the Garden of Eden (Genesis 3), used the uncircumcised Cyrus of Persia to liberate God's people Israel from the punishing Babylonian exile (Isaiah 44:24-45:8, Ezra 1:1-4; II Chronicles 36:22-23), and as jealous covenanting LORD God sacrificed God's only Son to rescue us sinful ingrates with forgiveness (Deuteronomy 6:4-15, Ephesians 2:1-10). So the dynamic within the Reformational christian Bible reading is not to be closeted in critical study, not quick on the evangelistic trigger, not pushy on one specific doctrine or premeditatedly subversive, ready to overthrow evil powers—that is God's work—but to posit, with prayerful reflection led by God's Spirit, in concert with the glossolalia all around us: to posit holy alternative ways to tend to God's world and introduce shalom into our broken-down society.

It takes time to read the Bible to hear God speak. The Bible is not a fast-food outlet. One has to pay attention to the written text, pore over it, learn the languages or consult several translations, deepen oneself into the original historical circumstances, piece out the literary features to catch the nuances, check a wide diversity of commentary readings on the particular text under scrutiny. Reading the Bible to hear God speak is not a one-person show—it happens best in a believing communion of attuned reading saints (often found in books!). Once prepared—led into a reading by those who know in faith better than yourself how to listen to the Bible—a person waits on the Lord, wrestles with the God-speaking text, and finally hears the Holy Spirit's voice of the text which humbles you to your knees with an oracle of tough love and rough comfort, and a mission of redemptive service. One never need say, "My prayers are not answered; God never talks to me," if you learn how to read the Bible to hear God speak. God speaks through the holy scriptures with mysterious clarity and empowering wisdom in a way that engenders faithfulness, patience, joy, trust, love, and hope.

* I am very grateful to Inès Naudin ten Cate-Seerveld, Robert Sweetman, and George Vandervelde for taking the careful time to check my writing of the Afterword, and for offering suggestions that made me, I hope, more clear, charitable, and responsible.

Notes

[1] Baruch A. Levine, *Numbers 1-20* (1993), *Numbers 21-36* (2000), Anchor Bible 4A,4B (Garden City: Doubleday & Co., Cf. also Hedwige Rouillard, *Le Péricope de Balaam* (Nombras 22-24). La prose et les 'oracles.' (Paris: Librairie Lecoffre, 1985); and Walter Gross, Bileam. *Literar- und formkritische Untersuchung der Prosa in Number 22-24* (München: Kösel Verlag, 1974).

[2] Marvin H. Pope on *The Song of Songs* (Anchor Bible 7C, 1977) treats six pages of Hebrew text with about 700 pages of research on mid-Eastern fertility cults, completely misreading the book that criticizes Solomon's lascivious old age recounted in I Kings 9-11. (Cf. my *The Greatest Song, in critique of Solomon* [Toronto Tuppence Press, 1988]). Mitchell Dahood in the Anchor Bible *Psalms* (3 volumes, 16,17,17A, 1966-1990) also expertly pinpoints technical features of the original text, but seldom lets the psalm rend our heart (cf. Joel 2:12-14), as if we do not need to hear, repent, and believe the LORD who is speaking to us in these scriptures. As editor Sugirtharajah says in "Postscript" to *Voices from the Margin*: "Historical criticism tends to introduce into the task of interpretation a division of labour between the exegete and the expositor, between the scholar and the preacher, and between biblical scholarship and theological enterprise. This is the original sin of the historical-critical method" (p.436).

[3] Cf. Craig A. Bartholomew, section on "The case for a christian hermeneutic," in *Reading Ecclesiastes, Old Testament exegesis and hermeneutical theory* (Roma: Editrice Pontifico Istituto Biblico, 1998), pp. 207-212. "Especially appeals for a church hermeneutic seem to me in danger of short-circuiting the philosophical scaffolding of a hermeneutic" (209 n.9).

[4] Editors Carol A. Newsom and Sharon H. Ringe state in *Women's Bible Commentary*, Expanded edition (Louisville: Westminster John Knox Press, 1998): "What contributors have selected includes not only portions of the Bible that deal explicitly with female characters and symbols but also sections that bear on the condition of women generally" (p. xxiv). Cf. also Elsa Tamez, "Women's Rereading of the Bible," in *Voices from the Margin*, pp. 61-70. David Gunn, who accepts the consequences, is quite forceful in his contribution to *A Feminist Companion to Reading the Bible: Approaches, methods and strategies*, eds. Athalya Brenner and Carole Fontaine (Sheffield: Academic Press, 1997): "I find it very hard to see where feminist criticism of the Bible can go 'constructively' without it destroying traditional notions of the Bible's authority as a sacred text" (p.564).

[5] Katherine Doob Sakenfeld in "Numbers," *Women's Bible Commentary*, Expanded edition, pp. 50, 52.

[6] This particular dogmatically filtered liberationist reading has been gleaned from several sources like the following: Walter Brueggemann, "Trajectories in Old Testament Literature and the Sociology of Ancient Israel," in *The Bible and Liberation: Political and social hermeneutics*, ed. Norman K. Gottwald Maryknoll: Orbis Books, 1983), pp. 307-333; *Voices from the Margin: Interpreting the Bible in the Third World*, ed. R.S. Sugirtharajah (Maryknoll: Orbis Books, 1991); Leif E. Vaage, "Introduction" to *Subversive Scriptures: Revolutionary readings of the christian bible in Latin america*, ed. L.E. Vaage (Valley Forge: Trinity Press International, 1997), pp. 1-23; *Return to Babel: Global perspectives on the Bible*, eds. Priscilla Pope-Levison and John R. Levison (Louisville: Westminster John Knox Press, 1999).

Various writers in the Gottwald edited book are explicit on their dogmatic intentions: Kuno Füssel says, "a materialist reading of the Bible … will help us find in the writings of the Old and New Testament hitherto undiscovered paradigms of a subversive practice" (p. 140 in "The Materialist Reading of the Bible: Report on an alternative approach to biblical texts," pp. 134-46); Rudolf J. Siebert writes that "critical sociologists of religion read the Bible as a subversive and revolutionary book" (p. 498 in "Jacob and Jesus: Recent Marxist readings of the Bible," pp. 397-517).

[7] Quotes in this section are taken from (1) the preface to *The Living Bible*, and (2) a speech by William F. Kerr before the Evangelical Theological Society in 1974 that was reproduced as an unpaginated advertisement in *Christianity Today*, 19 (no. 17, 23 May 1975):29-40. Cf. also Robert G. Bratcher, "One Bible in Many Translations," *Interpretation* 32:2 (April 1978):115-129; and David E. Garland on "The Living Bible" in *Review and Expositor* 76 (1979):387-408.

[8] The "Angel of the LORD" (*mal'ak Yahweh*) identifies his voice with that of the Lord God in Numbers 22:35, and that is a pivotal moment in the Balaam story. Christian readers have often thought that *mal'ak Yahweh* is an Older Testament way of referring to the presence of the second person of the Trinity before Christ's incarnation. Al Wolters is hesitant to accept this reading because in his judgment it "takes insufficient account of the redemptive-historical distance between Old and New Testament" ("Confessional Criticism and the Night Visions of Zechariah," *Renewing Biblical Interpretation*, p. 111).

[9] Robert Sweetman would distinguish from the Philo and Origen praxis the way Thomas Aquinas conceives of "plural senses in continuity with the literal sense" (*Summa Theologiae* 1.1.10), since the "spiritual senses" can embody the watershed of meaning natural to a faith community. Only a "modern" reader post-Spinoza need be uneasy with allegorical (Christ and the Church), moral (a saintly soul), and anagogic (the believers' intense, apocalyptic hope) senses of a biblical text, because the watershed of a faith-community has dried up.

Sweetman also shows how Thomas of Cantimpré pairs with his "scholarly" reading of biblical writings a "performative" reading which mode, it seems to me, points to what the Reformation thinkers and I call the kerygmatic nature of the Bible's historical-literal sense. Cf. Robert Sweetman, "Beryl Smalley, Thomas of Cantimpré and Performative Reading of Scripture: A study in two *Exempla*," in *With Reverence for the Word: Medieval Exegesis in Judaism, Christianity and Islam*, ed. Jane MacAuliffe, Barry Walfish, and Joseph Goering (Oxford: Oxford University Press, 2003, pp. 256-275).

Important to me is to claim, as Sweetman does too, that these two distinguished "readings" must not be compartmentalized and prioritized: **the Bible has this performative character as its nature** and thus can be and needs to harbour the kerygmatic dimension both outside of ecclesial confines and within the academic treatment of the biblical writings. Cf. below section (4).

[10] Cf. my "Proverbs 10:1-22: From poetic paragraphs to preaching," in *Reading and Hearing the Word: From text to sermon. Essays in honor of John H. Stek*, ed. Arie C. Leder (Grand Rapids: Calvin Theological Seminary, 1998): 181-200, and "Reading and Hearing the Psalms: The gut of the Bible," in *Pro Rege*, 27:4 (June 1999):20-32.

[11] Among the streams in which some of these thoughts were fished, in this Reformational section, are the following: Brevard S. Childs, "The *Sensus literalis* of Scripture: An ancient and modern problem," in *Beiträge zur Alttestamentlichen Theologie. Festschrift für Walther Zimmerli zum 70. Geburtstag*, eds. Herbert Donner, Robert Hanhart, Rudolph Smend (Göttingen: Vandenhoeck & Ruprecht, 1977), pp. 80-93; Bonnie Kittel, "Brevard Childs' Development of the Canonical Approach," in *JSOT*, 16 (1980):2-11; Hans W. Frei, "The 'Literal Reading' of Biblical Narrative in the Christian Tradition: Does it stretch or will it break?" in *The Bible and the Narrative Tradition*, ed. Frank McConnell (Oxford University Press, 1986), pp. 36-77; Garrett Green, "'The Bible as ... ': Fictional narrative and scriptural truth," in *Scriptural Authority and Narrative Interpretation* (Philadelphia: Fortress Press, 1987), pp. 79-96; M.G. Brett, "Literacy and Domination: G.A. Herion's sociology of history writing," in *JSOT*, 37 (1987):15-40; John Goldingay, *Models for Scripture* (Grand Rapids: William B. Eerdmans, 1994) and *Models for Interpretration of Scripture* (Grand Rapids: William B. Eerdmans, 1995); Donald Sinnema, "The Distinction between Scholastic and Popular: Andreas Hyperius and Reformed Scholasticism," in *Protestant Scholasticism: Essays in reassessment*, eds. Carl R. Trueman and R.S. Clark (Carlisle: Paternoster Press, 1999), pp. 127-143; Craig Bartholomew, "Uncharted Waters: Philosophy, theology and the crisis in biblical interpretation," in *Renewing Biblical Interpretation*, eds. C. Bartholomew, Colin Greene, Karl Möller (Carlisle: Paternoster Press, 2000), pp. 1-39; Raymond C. Van Leeuwen, "On Bible Translation and Hermeneutics," in *After Pentecost: Language and biblical interpretation* (Carlisle: Paternoster Press, 2001), pp.284-311.

[12] Cf. the *Belgic Confession* by Guido de Brès (1561-1566), articles 2-5; and my "The gospel of creation" [1978], *In the Fields of the Lord*, ed. Craig Bartholomew (Toronto Tuppence Press/Piquant, 2000), pp. 46-48; "Creational Revelation: God's glossolalia" [1990], appendix 1 in *Bearing Fresh Olive Leaves* (Toronto Tuppence Press/Piquant, 2000), pp. 159-163; "Reading the Bible like a Grown-up Child," *The Banner* 130:24 (26 June 1995):12-14.

Appendix

How Scripture relates to my professional academic work

1. The Bible operates in my scholarship the way the Bible operates in the rest of my life, like an iceberg.

2. I believe the Bible is Holy Scripture. This perspicuous canonic text telling the story of God's great deeds convicts me of what is true. Insofar as I hear God's voice aright, Scripture makes me wise.

   > "To stand still, listening before the Lord God gives you a head start in full-bodied knowledge, in wisdom, and in corrective discipline-exactly what fools despise" (Proverbs 1:7).

3. The head start the Bible provides for my (scholarly) life includes sanctifying direction on cosmic-historical horizons, my human place-and-task or fundamental calling before God in the Rule of Jesus Christ acoming, and the injunction to become reformingly holy (filled with the Holy Spirit) in my actual thought-life.

   > To add Scriptural information as "mental fodder" to unredeemed postulates or good intentions leads only to a deplorable synthesis (a synthetic christian product) which compromises the unblemished sacrifice God wants. Cf. John Kok, "Vollenhoven and Scriptural philosophy," *Philosophia Reformata*, 53:2 (1988):134 n.29.

4. Holy Scripture through God's Spirit has instructed me by a saving faith to know that the Creator God revealed in Jesus Christ is the sovereign Lord God of all creatures, justly commanding us sinful humans, "Love me with all your hearted corporeality."

   > Cf. Herman Dooyeweerd, "Why a radical christian philosophy can only develop in the line of John Calvin's religious starting-point," in *A New Critique of Theoretical Thought* [1935], translated 1953, 1:515-535f.

5. Further, the Bible (especially the Psalms and "Wisdom" books) has persuaded me of the vision that God's covenant with earthly (and heavenly) creatures is such that kinds of

individual entities are graciously subjected to ordinances for their gifted, responsible functioning in praise of the Lord together. The miraculous diversity of temporal creatures is unified by the Lord's Word in *theatrum Dei* of once-only, God-ordered duration-to-the-end.

Cf. John Kok, "Vollenhoven and Scriptural philosophy," on "principal themes of philosophy" consonant with Scripture; p. 133 n.28.

6. The Bible also speaks to me (in a community of scholarly saints too) that our (theoretical) life is vain unless the work of our hands/thinking be contributing to the redemptive/recreative work of Jesus Christ fleshed out by the Holy Spirit in Christ's historical body, restoring the original praise, edification, and care of creatures due the Lord (II Corinthians 5:17-19).

7. So the Holy Scriptures charter (cf. my *Rainbows for the fallen world*, chapter 1), provide over-all contours for, and spire the ministry of a thetical-critical, reconciling scholarship, viz., a Scripturally led philosophical systematics. Such an on-going, Reformational, Scripturally led philosophy needs to be embedded in a biblical Way-of-life and Scriptural world-and-life-vision shared by a community of saints, or the philosophical theory will become a cut flower. (The same holds true for christian artistry and worldview studies too.)

Cf. C. Seerveld, "Philosophy as schooled memory" [1982], *In the Fields of the Lord*, ed. Craig Bartholomew, 2000, pp. 84-89.

8. Because of the Scriptural format to my own philosophical perspective (in aesthetics), I can discern with my Junior members the troubles so many unScriptural philosophically loaded aestheticians and art theorists/critics/historians have in grasping the creatural/historical realities they are grappling with. We ask Scriptural philosophical questions, and listen intently for their (often brilliant, contorted) answers. In "anti-

sympathetic vibration" (*A Christian Critique of Art and Literature* [1963], rev. ed. 1995, p. 20) with such disobedient scholarly responses in our world which belongs to God, we followers of the Christ learn from their handicapped efforts, in order to reform our own Scripturally led analytic service.

9. Wrestling with the biblical text serves to focus me on being certain and faithful in my (professional) calling(s), and tends to protect me, I believe, from both fashionable problematics and ideology.

Presented as theses for discussion in a "Biblical Foundations" seminar at the Institute for Christian Studies, Toronto (February 1990).

Psalm 56

Song text by David for the cantor to the tune of "The silenced dove far, far away," written after the episode when the Philistines had him trapped in Gath (cf. I Samuel 21:10-22:1).

Be merciful to me, O God!
because people are chafing at the bit to hurt me,
all day long they press in viciously to mishandle me.
My enemies stalk me all day long,
yes, many of them highhandedly bully me!

On the day when I can't help but become afraid,
I still do somehow feel safe with You.
> *Near God I can still find cheer in what God is saying.*
> *With God I feel myself secure; I don't need to be afraid:*
> *what can mortal flesh do to me!*

[But] my antagonists give a nasty twist all the time to whatever I say;
everything that comes to their mind they slant it to be bad for me.
They provoke things, they lie in wait to ambush me;
they dog my footsteps like ones who are trying to end my life:
for such wicked harassment get rid of them [LORD]!
O God, in anger cut those people down to size!

[I know] You have kept track of my travail.
You personally collect [all] my tears in your wineskin bottle
—that's true, right!? they are all inscribed in your account book [of Life]!

So my enemies will be spun around backwards
on the day I cry out [to You] —
I know that with experiential certainty:
Yes, God does stand up for me!

With God, [whose] speaking I cherish,
with the Lord God [whose] word I revere:
with God I feel myself secure, trustworthily cared for,
I don't need to be afraid:
what could anybody human really do to me?!

The vows vowed to you, O God, weigh on me:
I should like to make good on songs of thanksgiving for You,
for You have rescued my life from a dead end!
That's right! You saved my feet from stumbling around [in circles]
so that I could walk to and fro [dance!] before the face of God
in the light of genuine living!

God Keeps My Tears in a Bottle

Psalm 56:8

Solo voice
Cm Gm Fm7 Cm
1 There's peo - ple out to hurt me bad. They
2 They dog my steps, pro - voke my life, and
3 I know, my Lord, You keep good track of
Gm Cm Fm7
men - ace, play the bul - ly. When I can't help but
twist my words to lies. O Lord! ex - pose their
all the pain and trou - ble, col - lect my tears like
Cm Gm7 1 & 3 Cm 2 Cm
be a - fraid, O God! pro - tect me ful - ly.
e - vil plans and cut them down to size!
bro - ken jewels and save them in a bot - tle.
Congregation (after stanzas 2 and 3)
Be mer - ci - ful to me, O God!
Solo voice
Dm Am Gm7 Dm
4 The en - e - mies shall be un - done the
5 What mor - tals can de - stroy my life!? The
6 It's time to of - fer thanks to You, to
Am Dm Gm7
day God hears my plea. I know with ut - ter
LORD God's Word is sure. I do not need to
dance be - fore your face. O God, You res - cued
Dm Em9 Dm
cer - tain - ty God does stand up for me!
be a - fraid: God's arms hold me se - cure.
me from death to live a life of grace!
Solo voice and congregation (after stanza 6 only)
Thank you for your mer - cy, Lord! A - men!

Text: Calvin Seerveld, © January, 2001
Tune: Calvin Seerveld, © 2001

87 87 with Refrain
GIOIA IN GOD'S BOTTLE BLUES

MY TEARS
GOD KEEPS
IN A BOTTLE
PSALM 56:8

(H) Joanne Sytsma, ***God keeps my tears in a bottle***
Psalm 56:8 (2001) Collection of the artist

This vivid oil painting on wood panel by Joanne Sytsma (b. 1941) surrounds a human person's tears and downcast eyes with the dumbfounding hope of a rainbow of colour. The grain of the wood appearing through the paint accentuates the feeling that the sorrowful face is awash with weeping. Yet the mouth turned funnel shows that the profoundest sadness of the faithful is channeled by the LORD into a safe blue bottle, where Matisse's "Dance of life" label tells what is in store for those crying in God's care (Psalm 30:11-12, Matthew 5:4, Luke 6:20-21). The sturdy cut-out letters and arrows of thick copper foil are a sure, sharp indication of God's fixed attention upon our pain and trouble.

List of illustrations

Brief Bibliography

A few worthwhile study sources

Alter, Robert. *The World of Biblical Literature*. New York: Basic Books, 1992.

Bartholomew, Craig and Colin Greene, Karl Möller, eds. *Scripture & Hermeneutic Series: Renewing Biblical Interpretation*. Grand Rapids: Zondervan, 2000. vol.1.

de Graaf, S.G. *Hoofdlijnen in de Inleiding tot het Nieuwe Testament*. Kampen: J.H. Kok, 1941.

de Graaf, S.G. *Verbondsgeschiedenis*. Kampen: J.H. Kok, 1952, 2 vols., translated by H. Evan and Elizabeth Runner as *Promise and Deliverance*. St. Catharines: Paideia Press, 1977-1981. 4 vols.

Evans, G.R. *The Language and Logic of the Bible: The earlier Middle Ages*. London: Cambridge University Press, 1984.

Flesseman-Van Leen, Ellen *ed. The Bible: Its authority and interpretation in the ecumenical movement*. Faith and Order Paper no. 99. Geneva: World Council of Churches, 1980.

Grant, Robert M. *A Short History of the Interpretation of the Bible* (1948), rev. ed. New York: Macmillan Co., 1963.

Hinson, E. Glenn ed. *Review and Expositor*, 76 (1979):299-416. Collection of articles that analyze putting the Bible into English, Revised Standard Version, New English Bible, The Jerusalem Bible, New American Standard Bible, New International Version, The Living Bible, The Good News Bible.

McConnell, Frank ed. *The Bible and the Narrative Tradition*. New York: Oxford University Press, 1986.

Newbingen, Leslie. *Truth and Authority in Modernity*. Valley Forge: Trinity Press International, 1996.

Seerveld, Calvin. *The Breath of God: The art of Bible translation*. 50 minute video, director David Christensen. Calgary/Toronto: Agitprop Films/Tuppence Press, 2001.

Smart, James D. *The Strange Silence of the Bible in the Church: A study in hermeneutics*. London: SCM Press, Ltd., 1970.

Spykman, Gordon J. "A Confessional Hermeneutic, alternative to the historical-critical method," *The Reformed Ecumenical Synod Theological Bulletin*, 1:3 (December 1973):1-13.

Spykman, Gordon J. *Reformational Theology: A new paradigm for doing dogmatics*. Grand Rapids: William B. Eerdmans, 1992.

Vanderwaal, Cornelis. *Sola Scriptura*, translated by Theodore Plantinga as *Search the Scriptures*. 10 vols., paperback. St. Catharines: Paideia Press, n.d.